Glasshouse

Greenhouse

India Hobson and
Magnus Edmondson
of Haarkon

PAVILION

First published in the United Kingdom in 2018 by
Pavilion
An imprint of HarperCollins*Publishers*
1 London Bridge Street
London SE1 9GF

www.harpercollins.co.uk

HarperCollins*Publishers*
Macken House
39/40 Mayor Street Upper
Dublin 1
D01 C9W8
Ireland

ISBN 978-1-911595-69-4

A CIP catalogue record for this book is available from the British Library.

10 9 8 7 6 5 4 3

Reproduction by Mission Productions Ltd
Printed and bound in China by RR Donnelley APS

THE HAARKON GREENHOUSE TOUR

A few years ago, and completely unbeknown to us, we embarked on a self-initiated greenhouse tour of the world. It began one cold morning in Oxford the day after we had photographed a wedding; we had decided to make a weekend of our trip south and saw it as a perfect excuse to get to know the city.

Sweeping vines flowed from the milky glass ceiling, emerald fingers stretched their leaves towards us and the air was thick with the scent of damp, warm earth. It had just turned 10 o'clock in the morning and we had found ourselves in the glasshouses at the University of Oxford Botanic Garden; we did not know it then, but we were hooked. Since that first visit a few years ago, we've wandered in countless other greenhouses; navigating our way through humble polytunnels, characterful cacti collections and tropical hothouses, travelling the world to seek out new plant-filled adventures.

People think that we are obsessed with plants, and we don't blame them for thinking that, but it's not really the case. Yes, we gravitate towards them and we have a healthy collection at home (over 100 in a one-bedroom apartment), but they are certainly not the be-all-and-end-all of our existence and, surprisingly enough, they are not the only reason for our interest in greenhouses.

Simply put, we are enthralled by these places where man and nature come together, and we find the connection between engineering and nature endlessly fascinating because there are so many ways in which the natural world is dealt with in design, and we love to see how people approach it. In composing our collection for this book we had to come up with what, in our eyes, defined a greenhouse and it was this:

The primary purpose of the structure must
be to house plant life.

We find beauty in the idea that someone would construct an entire building with the purpose of housing plant life; whether it is for research, crop cultivation or to display a proud collection, we believe the greenhouse to be the ultimate botanical pedestal.

Far from the concrete typologies of photographers Bernd and Hilla Becher, or the detailed botanical studies of Karl Blossfeldt, the Haarkon Greenhouse Tour is a more personal exploration and, as it turns out, a rather poetic ode to the humble plant house. You may find the odd factual snippet here, but it's much more about capturing the sentiment of the places that we visited, the essence of the greenhouses and the passion with which they have been created.

The majority of greenhouses we visit tend to be reimagined versions of their Victorian forefathers in esteemed botanical gardens, or lean-to vineries that nestle against the red brick walls of National Trust kitchen gardens. Whilst our interest in horticulture isn't quite advanced enough to discriminate from plant to plant just yet, we do find ourselves practising a little escapism, fantasizing about warmer climates, and therefore we lean in the direction of the tropics. Our own house is home to the 1970s classics; *Monstera deliciosa*, a tree-like *Schefflera* and various cacti and succulents, most of which are far too delicate to live beyond the warmth inside. Even our sun-trap of a patio is too harsh an environment for them and they find themselves huddled on shelves or, regrettably, gathered on the floor near the window. An indoor jungle is the ideal sanctuary for both them and us and can be enjoyed whatever the weather outside.

So far on our travels we have yet to find two greenhouses that are exactly the same. There doesn't seem to be an industry standard when it comes to their construction, and that playfulness in the architectural language is a huge part of their appeal. Frames of aluminium or wood are commonplace, while shapes vary from classic gable designs, to exotic domes and sci-fi-esque spaceships. We particularly like homemade versions – repurposed doors and unstable bricks that have lived a previous life. These tend to be a little wilder inside too, with tendrils searching for a fissure in the glass to taste the cold air beyond.

Character is further defined by the choice of planting and the manner in which it is undertaken. At one stage we would have said that the more exotic the better – a textbook case of wanting what we can't have, and as foliage is king in our world, it will come as no surprise that we think aroids, members of the arum family, are a pleasing sight. Aroids come in all shapes and sizes and the decoration on their leaves knows no bounds, with varying textures of gloss, leather and velvet. Now though, having

seen so many types and interpretations of the greenhouse, we take whatever comes, and as long as it brings personality and a voice, we will champion it. There's an underlying theme of future-proofing, of being aware of conservation and the importance of caring for the natural world that runs through this book, and that can show no discrimination from one plant species to another; all the plants, animals and other inhabitants of the Earth are paramount to its continuance and we have to be aware of that.

A common question we are asked is whether we have a single favourite glasshouse out of all those we have visited, and in all honesty, the answer is no. Although we will jump at the chance to marvel at the 1960s inside-out structures of the Royal Botanic Garden in Edinburgh (the supports of the building are designed to be on the outside, allowing more room for the plants inside – a notion that we absolutely can't argue with), and we have lost count of the hours we have spent exploring the Rainforest Biome at Eden Project, we truly think that variety is what makes the whole journey interesting for us. The highest indoor waterfall of the Cloud Forest in Gardens by the Bay in Singapore rendered us speechless, but the reclaimed-window allotment creation in Sheffield touched us equally; there really is no place in the greenhouse world for favourites and we have time for them all.

You will notice that we have divided the book into chapters and attempted to categorize our findings. We found this a particularly difficult task because in reality, all greenhouses can fit into each category, so don't take it too literally; just because we've put something into the Specimen section, it doesn't mean it is not appropriate for Pleasure too.

For us greenhouses, in whatever form, are a perfect marriage of man and nature; where the organic and the engineered become a little confused, mixed up and grow wild together, and we don't think we'll ever tire of losing an afternoon under a glass roof. We think this is time well spent.

Some Context

You will find that as you make your way through our tour that a) it usually rains wherever we go (which makes us even more thankful we chose a project about the *inside* gardens of the world), and b) many of the greenhouses take on a familiar form and will usually refer to Joseph Paxton's creations as an influence on their design. It makes sense therefore, before going further, for us to explain a little of his contribution to the world of glasshouse construction.

Paxton was born in 1803 and by the age of 15 had developed a keen interest in gardening, and worked in the garden at Battlesden Park, a large Manor House just outside Woburn in Bedfordshire. In 1823 he started a more senior position at Chiswick Gardens, which belonged to the Royal Horticultural Society. It was here that he made an impression on William Cavendish, the 6th Duke of Devonshire, who lived at Chiswick House not too far from the RHS garden. He quickly took a shine to Paxton and offered him the role of head gardener at Chatsworth House in Derbyshire – today we live just half an hour away from Chatsworth and often walk in Paxton's footsteps to gain a sense of his beginnings.

At Chatsworth, Paxton settled in easily and enjoyed the major tasks he was given, such as redesigning the formal gardens, creating an arboretum, building the rock garden and installing the Emperor Fountain – all of which are still in place today. He developed a love of engineering, and combined this with the Duke's quest to grow exotic fruits, such as pineapples and peaches. In those days the use of greenhouses was in its early stages, and although glasshouses did exist at Chatsworth, they were a little worse for wear and not really fit for purpose. Paxton took on the task of designing his own and for this he utilized the 'ridge and furrow' structure invented by (another greenhouse legend) John Claudius Loudon. The zig-zag of the roof allowed light and heat to come through the glass for as long as possible throughout the day, no matter which direction the sun was coming from, and with its glazed walls the building provided protection from the wind and rain, allowing the environment inside to be almost completely controlled.

The next project given to Paxton was the cultivation of what was originally known as *Victoria regia*, or more commonly known as the Amazon waterlily. Sent as a seed from Kew in 1836, and originally brought back from an expedition to the Amazon itself, there was a race to be the first to cultivate the lily and Joseph Paxton went all out in his attempt to be the winner. He entrusted the seed to his junior and within two months a telegram had been sent to Queen Victoria to let her know that the lily had produced a flower and the race was well and truly over. If you're not familiar with the *Victoria amazonica* (as it is now known), the lily pads can grow to over 10ft (3m) in length, and therefore require a large body of water in which to live. As a result Paxton set about building a greenhouse dedicated solely to the waterlily in the form of the Great Conservatory on the south side of Chatsworth House. Paxton looked to the plant itself to research his design for the glasshouse, and specifically the underside of the huge leaves, noting the veins that radiate from the centre of the leaf. More than just decorative, these ribs provide the plant with rigidity and strength, and the same principles were carried forward into the Great Conservatory. Paxton built the glasshouse (sometimes also referred to as the 'stove') with a cast-iron frame, supplemented by laminated wood for the curves and a whopping 7 miles (11.3km) of pipes provided the heating. It also required custom sheet glass to be made.

Unfortunately the conservatory was far too expensive to heat continuously, and after switching off the heating during the First World War a great number of plants died, and the glasshouse was demolished; now there is a maze in its place.

Following his initiation at Chatsworth, Paxton continued on a glasshouse quest by securing the job of designing the Crystal Palace for The Great Exhibition of 1851. This is probably the most famous glasshouse in history despite the fact that it was destroyed by fire in 1936. The Crystal Palace was regarded as a masterpiece of engineering and a demonstration of the innovative industrial technologies available at the time, built using pre-fabricated components, and Paxton was knighted for his efforts.

We have stood in many greenhouses, Victorian and otherwise, and looked up to see that familiar waterlily leaf design forming the structure of the roof, and we like knowing that it is a little nod to Paxton – and the desire to grow exotic plants in places where they shouldn't be able to grow.

HISTORY

HORTUS BOTANICUS

Amsterdam, The Netherlands

Our visits to Hortus Botanicus always seem to coincide with fresh early mornings when the sun is still low in the Amsterdam sky, and the condensation fogs up the glass from the inside. The unmistakable hexagonal pyramids of the tropical house glisten as they come into our view from across the canal and bring promises of exotic lands a world away from the cold chill in the air on the quiet street outside. The proximity to the city is pretty special; most of our botanical adventures involve multiple bus or train rides and long walks into suburbs, or sometimes even further, but not here. It is a true retreat from the crowds that spill into every other corner of the capital city.

Inside the glasshouse we find ourselves elevated on a treetop walkway and can look down on the shrubs and trees that are native to the slightly warmer climes of the Mediterranean.

The steel pathway leads you further upwards and converging lines throw themselves across our field of vision, all pointing towards the steamy entrance ahead of us.

The automatic doors open and we find ourselves entering the tropical portion of the building at a height. From our vantage point up here we are right in the middle of the action; cycad palms and *Pandanus* (from places quite close to the equator) form the height of the 'jungle' and act as supports for the climbers that follow the trunks up to the top of the canopy where they can find more light. As we descend the stairs, we feel the jungle swallow us a little more with each step, and eventually we find ourselves on the 'forest' floor among Wandering Jew (*Tradescantia*), Bird's Nest Fern (*Asplenium*) and many types of *Anthurium* and *Philodendron* with their heart-shaped leaves.

A pond that appears almost black sits in the centre of the room, reflecting the graphic linear patterns of the ceiling framework, and if we look for long enough we can see terrapins moving slowly, if at all. The walkways in the tropical room ripple and wind around the pond, occasionally leading us onto smaller paths laden with bark, right through the jungle and back again until we're not sure if we've seen it from that aspect before or not.

The third climate that the glasshouse provides is the desert, and that features in the adjacent room. A long wall painted in tones of pink, salmon and terracotta spans the back of the room and serves as a background to the cacti and *Euphorbia* that stand in front. The air is noticeably drier in here and everything seems much clearer in front of our eyes compared to the humidity of before. If we squint, we can pretend that the colour of the wall is a Californian sunset (we've got great imaginations because, thankfully, it is not quite as hot as the actual desert), and the greeny-blue hues of *Agave* come into their own. It's a combination that has become very familiar to us via the Instagram account #PlantsOnPink that we see so much in our digital lives.

The desert is a place that brings out the true fighters in the plant world and here we can see many textures that neither of us really wants to come into contact with. Spines grab at us as we walk by, cacti covered in fluffy white cotton (or so it appears) and juicy-looking succulents are dotted around the dry, rocky *terra firma*.

The return journey back through the jungle is just as interesting as it was on the way in, only this time the view is different, as we notice vibrant, acid-green fan palms that we are sure weren't there before. We walk past plants belonging to the ginger family (Zingiberaceae) that will bear bright red and orange flowers once the weather warms a little, a glass case of delicate orchids and last, but not least, a display of air plants that sit along planks on a washing line by the window. The automatic doors pull back and we are reluctantly led back into the cooler temperatures that prepare us for the early spring outdoors.

THE NURSERY GREENHOUSES

Forde Abbey and Gardens, Somerset, UK

A screenshot of the wilderness at Forde Abbey had long been on our minds before we investigated it in person, but we managed to combine a flying visit with a Dorset holiday and we are hugely glad that we did so. As always, the rain was pouring, and we were totally ill-prepared for being outdoors, so we dodged around the puddles as best we could in an effort to avoid being completely drenched as we made our way from the car park to the rather imposing oak door at the front of the house – a former Cistercian monastery that has existed since the 1100s. We are not quite sure why our natural way of dealing with rain is to duck our heads as deeply as we can into our shoulders, but it definitely doesn't work and we were utterly soaked by the time our host welcomed us into the warmth and comforting darkness of Forde Abbey.

The Abbey has a rich (and quite complicated) history of residents, from monks to politicians, as well as a philosopher, and now serves as the private residence of the Roper family, who have been custodians of the house since the early 1900s. The Ropers open the house to paying visitors, wedding ceremonies and film crews throughout the year, and of course to interested parties like ourselves who can't pass a property without peering over the fence at the gardens and outbuildings …

The gardens at Forde Abbey are rather special and appear on the National Heritage List for England with a Grade II* listing due to their historical significance. We were told about the arboretum, topiary-lined lawns and saw a glimpse of colour in the walled garden, although the rain certainly muddied our view – but gave us yet one more reason to go back.

Our journey to the garden doubled as a tour of the house and we were guided through great halls and corridors, shown rooms of opulent grandeur (but not so palatial that we couldn't imagine living there ourselves) and of course the iconic cloisters that look so much better in real life than on a tiny handheld screen.

Although a conversation took place about whether to include the cloisters themselves as part of our tour, we felt that as such, the purpose of the architecture was intended for something other than plant life, and so our attention moved to the Victorian walled kitchen garden at the rear of the main house.

Probably the most common type of greenhouse still standing in the UK, the walled garden greenhouse is typical of the large manor houses that are scattered over the British countryside, and we have become rather familiar with their formation. Usually attached to the red brick wall that lines the garden, a greenhouse would protrude outwards with a sloping or curved roof that meets another, lower brick wall on the other side. In most cases a cog system integrated into the ironwork of the window frames controls the opening and closing of the windows, and in the more advanced examples a boiler and pipe system runs throughout the houses to keep them warm during the winter months.

It feels as if we have seen hundreds of these, and although there are some that are really quite lovely – Clumber Park and Calke Abbey are just two examples – the range at Forde Abbey won us over hands down. The deciding factor is the life that lies within and which in this case is quite literally bursting out. We love the feral inclination of one particular section of the greenhouses, and it is that of a nursery owner who has the kind permission of the Roper family to base his small horticulture business here, selling herbaceous perennials and textured grasses.

This glasshouse is where the inside and outside become blurred and every broken window pane serves as a spectacular viewing aperture into the next room as well as a passageway along which foliage can travel. We much prefer the untamed atmosphere to the manicured aesthetic of other places, but can appreciate that it might not be the most efficient use of space, although that really does depend on your intentions …. We chose the greenhouses at Forde Abbey as an example of a typical Victorian kitchen garden for its pure underdog qualities, and who doesn't love a good underdog?

CONSERVATORY OF FLOWERS

San Francisco, California, USA

We had just two days in San Francisco but couldn't pass up a chance to visit the Conservatory of Flowers. Not normally flower enthusiasts (we usually shy away from bright colours), we were intrigued by this conservatory and its resilience, and we managed to tear ourselves away from the chilled-out atmosphere of the Outer Sunset neighbourhood and spend a few hours with a conservatory veteran.

Situated inside Golden Gate Park (we hadn't quite anticipated how huge the park was as we'd spent so long looking at maps on the Internet that our sense of scale had deserted us altogether),

the Conservatory of Flowers was one of the first municipal conservatories constructed in the USA, and is still the oldest wooden municipal conservatory in the country; it is certainly the largest wooden building we see on our greenhouse tour. The fact that it is constructed from wood may not seem all that remarkable at first, but when you consider it was completed in 1879, survived a fire, an earthquake, countless storms, another fire and years of neglect, it seems that perhaps it is more of a miracle than a glasshouse; when we learned of its eventful life it gave us a newfound respect for the building.

The origins of the structure are a little muddy as no primary records of the component parts have been discovered, but we do know that the Conservatory of Flowers came to San Francisco by happy accident. The short version of its history is that a wealthy businessman, James Lick, bought the conservatory in kit form with the intention of having it at his home in Santa Clara. Following Lick's death in 1876, the trustees of his estate sold the kit to Leland Stanford (the founder of Stanford University) and Charles Crocker (the founder of the Central Pacific Railroad), together with 25 other business and community leaders of note, who donated it as a gift to the City of San Francisco. American greenhouse and boiler manufacturer Lord Burnham (the company also responsible for the design of the glasshouse in The New York Botanical Garden a few years later, see page 128) put the kit together, including its 16,800 window panes, and two tons of putty in the frames to keep the glass in place.

Aside from its unwavering determination to remain standing, we chose to include the Conservatory of Flowers in this book for one room – or 'gallery' as they are known – that we felt had particular charm: the Aquatic Plants Gallery. It is here that the wonderful ornateness comes shining through as the curls and loops of the architecture are mirrored beautifully in the tendrils and hanging vines of the plant life within.

The raised tanks are filled to the brim with deep, black water, and floating on the surface are the familiar leaves of waterlilies, with the occasional pink-tinged flower showing its face. We appreciated the arching growth of the pale leaves that make their way along the sweeping lines of the domed roof, and hang down over the water, thick with texture and plentiful life. Carnivorous plants such as *Nepenthes* are here too, their fleshy, funnel-shaped bodies decorated in greens, reds and purples like galaxies captured by the Hubble Space Telescope, lingering patiently for insects to become their lunch. The waves and curls of the pitcher plants almost exactly match the lines of the greenhouse structure and we find that relationship very pleasing indeed.

The aims and intentions of the Conservatory of Flowers are clear and concise: to 'connect people and plants in a place of exceptional beauty', and we think that they are entirely successful in their mission.

NY CARLSBERG GLYPTOTEK WINTER GARDEN

Copenhagen, Denmark

Copenhagen is a city of architecture and we spent four days in the summer getting acquainted with some of the breathtaking design with which Denmark has become synonymous. We tiptoed the aisles of Grundtvig's Church, walked in the footsteps of architect Finn Juhl at his house in Charlottenlund, and sat in all of the famous chairs at the Design Museum. It is a city with many faces and styles that are so quintessentially Danish, although altogether different from one another. We saw unwavering straight lines, smooth surfaces and immaculate finishes alongside brickwork so fine and so dainty that elves (known as 'nisser' in Denmark) could have laid it – all in a palette of ochre, amber and a steely blue-grey to match the moody sky above.

At golden hour after a day of tireless flânerie, we were surprised by the tranquillity of the conservatory just inside the Ny Carlsberg Glyptotek Museum. Enclosed in a setting of marble columns, terrazzo floors and intricately painted ceilings, the Winter Garden provides a botanical softness and a change of pace to everything else we had seen thus far in Denmark's capital. The entrance of the museum, designed and built in 1897 by Danish architect Vilhelm Dahlerup, is a cavernous dark space that changes our bodies into silhouettes, like three-dimensional versions of an Athenian vase. Stepping from the darkness into the light, bright, 1906 conservatory addition, we look up to the domed roof and marvel at the converging lines that meet in the sky; lilac on one side and a dazzling gold on the other in the evening sunshine. Here, in an indoor/outdoor union, we indulge in the rare treat of just being able to sit and be still for a while.

The Winter Garden has quite a romantic feel to it compared to other Danish architecture that we'd encountered; it is all fine lines and delicate curves, extra decoration wherever possible and a real touch of elegance through the *fleurs-de-lis* on the walls and mosaic flooring throughout. Marble statues sprawl and pirouette on their plinths, performing a slow dance with the palms, complemented by a supporting cast of deep green philodendrons.

Ny Carlsberg Glyptotek ('glypto' from the Greek root *glyphein* 'to carve', and *theke* meaning 'storing place') came about during the late 19th century, when art collector and brewer (of Carlsberg Brewery fame) Carl Jacobsen ran out of room to house his private sculpture collection, after exhausting his 19 galleries and taking over his own conservatory at home. He founded the museum and commissioned the design and build in Dahlerup's historicist style, and his fondness of the classical Roman arts is plain to see, not only in the building itself but in the artwork displayed within it. The museum comprises a small family of galleries, including a recent extension that plays with the storytelling of the building's growth and development, and around 10,000 artworks and artefacts that are permanent residents here. We love that Jacobsen had such a fondness for plant life that he approached it in much the same way as his antiquities; he immortalized them in a vitrine and displayed them as nature's own expression, asking visitors to the museum to look upon each leaf as they would an oil painting or the Rodin figures that line the hall.

As we don't own our own greenhouse, it is a rare thing to be able to sit inside one at the end of the day when most visitors have dispersed, and so this occasion seemed particularly important to us; surrounded by the soft evening glow and Latin we didn't understand, we found some welcome moments of contemplation and quiet repose.

SPECIMEN

MOORTEN
BOTANICAL GARDEN

Palm Springs, California, USA

Palm Springs was the first stop on our jaunt through California and we felt that everywhere seemed slightly empty. We were convinced that our hotel had opened its doors just for us as we were the only ones in the pool, the only ones in the diner at breakfast and a similar theme continued throughout our entire stay. It was only when we ventured out to see the mid-century architecture that we realized why no one was around; it was the middle of August with a searing, dry heat of 104°F (40°C) – we didn't see anyone because we were the only ones foolish enough to be walking around.

Nestled beneath the San Jacinto Mountains is a very special garden and one that's been around since the 1950s. It is not necessarily the most conventional of stop-off points for tourists, but it is a place that is renowned in Palm Springs, and certainly topped our 'must-see' list.

It is a place alive with over 3,000 crawling cacti that have been lovingly collected and nurtured here, originally by Chester Moorten, a retired actor and contortionist, together with his wife Patricia (a biologist), and now championed by their son Clark. The Moortens moved to Palm Springs where they built an arboretum and nursery that focused on cacti and other desert plants. Under Clark's care, and no doubt in large part because of social media, the specialist plant nursery has become world famous, and we can see why.

As our focus is on greenhouses, and with the red-hot sun beating down, we sweep past the *Agave*, *Euphorbia* and *Bombax* that live outdoors, and head excitedly towards the yellowing building we can see on the far side of the garden. Arriving at the rear of the structure (that reminds us a little of Second World War Anderson air-raid shelters) we see the masterpiece of the Moorten Botanical Garden in the form of 'The World's First Cactarium' (as the sign says). It's a low-tech affair, but packs a punch in terms of character once you step inside, and is one of only a few greenhouses we've been to that have to be cooled rather than heated. Our entry is delayed slightly by a fashion shoot, and we watch as the models pose nonchalantly in front of the tangled backdrop of hanging cacti, trying to show off the cuffs of their bell-sleeved blouses by reaching out to touch the spines of the cacti.

We note that the light that enters through the domed corrugated shell turns a subtle but slightly sickly green colour and falls evenly on everything inside. The building materials for the internal beds are crude and rather basic, but that is their brilliance and we commend the use of such simplistic design. It makes us want to run to our DIY store as soon as we get home. The aisles are clean and clear, obviously very well kept, and all the plants have their own setting in the sandbanks with handwritten labels that bring a really personal touch.

There are no colourful and informative panels to explain the displays, no child-friendly treasure hunt to find giant fibreglass animals, and not a single QR code in sight; instead we are here just for joy and pleasure, and to see the legacy of a private collection that we can view for a $5 entrance fee. We love the wildness and the personality here and can only wish the same for our own collection.

GLASSHOUSES

Chelsea Physic Garden, London, UK

The 3¾ acres (1.5ha) of elegantly planted garden have been close to the bank of the River Thames at Chelsea Physic Garden since 1673, long before Kew was established, and it was even longer before we found our way there for the first time, one grey day at the end of the summer. Reading the history of the garden is a bit like reading a *Harry Potter* book, as it is full of words like 'worshipful society', 'herbarium' and 'apprentice', but to summarize, it was set up as a garden for the early Apothecaries, and grew plants with healing and medicinal properties. A member of the London Museums of Health and Medicine, and now a registered charity, it opened its doors to the public for the first time in 1983.

It is said that England's first ever greenhouse was built here, but there is no primary evidence to support that. What we do know is that the opulent ochre glasshouses now standing have been at Chelsea Physic Garden since 1902, and they are a neat little group made from the most sumptuous Burmese teak. Having survived two World Wars completely unscathed, they are shining examples that, when cared for, wooden frames can stand the test of time – of course it helps that they're nestled snugly into the surrounding brick wall of the garden and therefore sheltered from anything that might be thrown their way, weather or otherwise. A solid fuel-heated Stove House was built at the centre of the site in 1680 to provide additional warmth to the plants inside. This was advanced technology for the time, and allowed the gardeners to control the temperature and ventilation, enabling them to grow new, more fragile, plant species, such as citrus fruits, all year round. The Stove House has since been demolished to make way for the development of the garden, but with poetic names like The Garden of Edible and Useful Plants, how can we object?

Inside, the glasshouses are divided into regions, but in a way that is less familiar than we are accustomed to; there is the House of Atlantic Islands, the Pelargonium House and the Southern Hemisphere House, and one that really piques our imagination – the Tropical Corridor. In all the houses, the floor space and movement of visitors is somehow secondary to the collections (this is by no means a criticism!), with potted specimens filling the tables, and occasionally spilling onto the floor, sometimes blocking the way. We love that aeoniums are given a voice here, and they are really quite impressive to look at, cared for with impeccable attention to detail with not a withered leaf in sight.

The Tropical Corridor is precisely that. It is not a glasshouse in its own right, but a passageway that has been utilized to its full extent with a temperature of over 59°F (15°C) throughout the year. It is humid and receives light for most of the day through the glass roof, so the plants in here are native to the tropics, with a huge number of them being edible: coffee, papaya, black pepper and rice. We were fortunate enough to be present when a cacao pod was harvested and it is quite lovely to know that somewhere there is a bar of chocolate with Chelsea Physic's name on it.

A wander around the garden reveals other greenhouses; the Thomas Moore Fernery, which is a vision in white and full to the brim with, of course, ferns. Near the fernery is a Cactus House that stands out to us as it appears to be a lean-to extension – much like those adjacent to countless homes around the UK. Great steps of bright orange are built up into the body of the greenhouse, and sitting on each ledge is a gaggle of terracotta pots, chattering with cacti and succulents. The interior is dominated by the painted edges of the shelving, and though a little garish, it is a colour that works – especially when paired with the various greens and blues of the plants. It is places like this that make us really happy; they are the unsung heroes and the underdog gardens, quietly doing what they do with no hue and cry, instead carving out a reputation for excellence. We are always met with a warm reception at Chelsea Physic, and the fact that it is the size it is makes it delightful, and perhaps even *achievable*.

THE CAMELLIA HOUSE

Yorkshire Sculpture Park,
West Yorkshire, UK

If somebody described this building to us we would probably dismiss it as too traditional for our liking. We are at home in the presence of Modernist and Brutalist architecture, and are usually attracted to clean, functional buildings made of wood, steel and concrete. The Grade II-listed Camellia House at Bretton Hall in Wakefield is an entirely different kettle of (greenhouse) fish, and on paper it's not really 'us'.

But photographing a wedding here one summer's day, we changed our minds. We have been inside the Camellia House dozens of times, but after capturing a bride and groom during their post-ceremony high, we felt the need to revisit for ourselves the next day and the forecast promised a similar spell of afternoon sun. Although all our previous wanders through the house had been slightly softer underfoot (when camellias are in flower they tend to carpet the floor with bright pink petals as the buds explode), this time the trees were decorated only with the warm glow of the afternoon light.

Built around 1812 for Colonel Thomas Richard and his wife Diana Beaumont, the Camellia House was designed by a man named Jeffry Wyatt (later Wyattville). A full heating system was constructed, however, a couple of years after completion, it was discovered that camellias (native to Eastern and Southern Asia) had no need of extra protection from the British weather, and would survive a winter quite happily outdoors. Nevertheless, the thick stone body of the building was filled with camellias, and still stands strong today with a fine collection of rich, glossy-leaved trees. For a building designed specifically for a certain plant, we think it is quite amusing that it provides protection that is wholly unnecessary, and as a result the whole thing becomes a showcase or a focal point of Bretton Hall's garden, much like the monuments and follies championed by Capability Brown just a century before.

It becomes less about the camellias inside, and more about the action of moving between the walls. The interior layout means that we inevitably walk each aisle and ensure we've covered each pathway – just in case there is a corner that we haven't inspected – and therefore we know we haven't missed out on anything. Typical of most buildings of the era it boasts full-height windows and presents its natural inhabitants symmetrically, integrating arched bays in the corners with a criss-cross of straight lines in the trellis that traverses along the walls. It is a meeting of man and nature, with a foot firmly in the past, which seems to cause time to pause for a while.

TATTON PARK FERNERY

Knutsford, Cheshire, UK

The fernery at Tatton Park is a wonderful place; the Grade II-listed L-plan box is accessed via a smaller greenhouse, which is full of geraniums and cyclamen and other bright, decorative flowers, or at least it is every time we go. A heavy white door set in the painted brick wall is a sort of secret entrance, the only clue to what's inside is provided by a rogue piece of ivy that has crept its way through the gap between the door and the frame, and is now making its way up the side of the wall.

A paved pathway, just one person wide, leads us into the fernery and blue *Agapanthus* fireworks burst in our peripheral vision. That powder blue is the only colour here aside from variations of green and the deep brown-black of the tree trunks. The walls inside are stepped upwards and lined with tree ferns so that we feel as if we are deep within the Earth, or in a sunken garden wrapped in geothermal energy. The way the plants rise up envelops us, trapping us inside a prehistoric kingdom, ruled by greenery that has formed a protective layer over the top of the soil and any other surface in the vicinity. The greens are layered on top of one another: the vibrant acid colour of *Selaginella* and moss that coats the undergrowth and the brighter stars of *Asplenium*; upwards through fanned fronds of bracken; and finally in the form of the feathery canopy that is silhouetted against the glass roof.

In Britain in the 1830s the general public became increasingly interested in botany. This extended to lesser-known plant life and by the 1850s, Pteridomania (or Fern-Fever) spread across Victorian England, and infiltrated British culture in the fields of fashion, the decorative arts, interiors and, of course, home horticulture. From professionals to amateurs alike, the Victorians filled their homes with pressed leaves and live plants, and created outdoor collections to display their love of the ferns to the world. In 1839, Nathaniel Bagshaw Ward designed a carrying device known as the Wardian Case that made transportation and display an easy task and these are echoed today in our use of terrariums to create a portable microclimate in our homes.

The Wardian Case was a tool used extensively in the early days of greenhouses and botanical exploration, as it allowed delicate plants to be carried from exotic locations around the world, and brought back to England for study and appreciation. Prior to the development of the Wardian Case, specimens were often brought back as seeds, or unsuccessfully as live examples. In the instance of Tatton Park, the extensive collection of ferns was gathered from New Zealand and Australia by Captain Charles Randle Egerton whose family lived at Tatton Hall from the late 16th century until it was bequeathed to the National Trust in 1958.

Though the fernery at Tatton Park wasn't built until 1859, glasshouses have existed in the park grounds since the 1700s, and were used to cultivate fruits that couldn't be grown outside in England, such as pineapples, figs, grapes, apricots and peaches. Designed by greenhouse genius Joseph Paxton and his apprentice G.H. Stokes, the fernery is a red-brick building with a glass topper, supported by a cast iron frame. As well as the fernery, the park is also home to a conservatory (known as the Pinery Vinery) show house, Peach House, Fig House, Orchid House and a Tomato House. We favour the fernery for a number of reasons. One is that we think it is quite a rarity to see a dedicated fern house, despite their popularity a century or two ago – we find that a

number of historic greenhouses have been removed or replaced due to their deterioration, or simply because the land they occupy was more lucrative for the owner if used for a different purpose. It is certainly true that now we can travel in person to see plants that we can't grow at home, and of course supermarkets are packed to the rafters with produce from all over the world. We like that the roof had to be raised higher in order to house the towering tree ferns (*Dicksonia*), and that when inside we are immersed in absolute greenery, with no other colour to rival our attention. Interestingly, ferns aren't like other plants, because they don't have flowers or seeds, but instead reproduce from spores and something called a gametophyte, and can only

do so in areas that are rich in moisture and shade. It's a niche that we really like and we appreciate that many decades ago someone felt the same – enough to build a whole house for them to live in with a heating system running throughout.

Ferns are among the oldest plants recorded on Earth with the earliest dating from the Devonian period (about 360 million years ago), but most of the species around today date from about 145 million years ago, during the Cretaceous period. This means we can't help but think of the connection between the greenery here and the history of the Earth as a whole; standing in the fernery we are looking back on time itself and making connections with the past.

ORCHID WORLD

Barbados

The Caribbean island of Barbados is probably the last place that we would expect to find an addition to our tour but here we certainly did. We may have relaxed the rules slightly on our definition of 'greenhouse' for this one, but we felt it was important to include because when we sat down to consider everything, it actually meets more of our criteria than we realized.

Located in a beautifully rich and colourful garden that covers an 8 acre (3.2ha) site on a Barbadian hillside, the gardens at Orchid World are totally tropical. We visited in the height of summer and found the heat and humidity to be overwhelming at times – the shade of the huge plantain leaves was much welcomed and we took every opportunity available to find an escape from the sweltering sun.

Lush palms of all descriptions fill our field of vision with striped trunks and all the colours from the middle of the rainbow; from vibrant and zingy oranges to near-fluorescent greens, leaves glowing vivaciously in the midday sun. At the foot of a winding path, a small waterfall flows into a pool of teal water that is surrounded by the heart-shaped leaves of *Philodendron* and starbursts of elegant *Cyperus*. A series of orchid houses (one with a sign on the door that reads, 'Orchid Hospital') and a grotto made of coral – the material from which the entire island is formed – sit on the lower boundary of the garden, and on the other side of a fence sugar cane stretches out until it reaches a bank of dense jungle.

The orchids are held in their cages like precious jewels in a museum, suspended from wires and trailing their pendulous roots below them. Few plants are actually in flower when we visit, and we learn that some of the specimens flower for only a couple of days a year, so we were lucky to see those that we did, and even more lucky that they happened to be in a colour palette that we were comfortable with – neutral tones will forever be our comfort zone.

At the top of the hill, a gruelling uphill climb in the 95°F (35°C) heat, perches a simple structure painted acid green to blend in with its surroundings. It is linear, and not much more substantial than the cages we had just seen, but it is a building nonetheless. It has

been assembled using simple materials: concrete blockwork enveloping an internal scaffold frame, with timbers to raise the roof and plastic sheeting to cover it; the whole thing has an agricultural feel. Fine netting is stretched across it to let the air flow freely while keeping out large birds and other animals (in fact aphids are the main predator but there is not much that can be done to stop those getting in). We like the honesty of this particular greenhouse – which is the opposite to almost every other candidate in our collection – built for keeping the temperatures from soaring by providing shade, whereas most of our other greenhouses provide warmth in the absence of the heat of the sun.

T.H. EVERETT
ALPINE HOUSE

Wave Hill, New York, USA

We found the garden at Wave Hill to be an absolute gem. Modest in size but still a world larger than any garden we are likely to own. There is a view of the Hudson River from the jam-packed raised gardens, and a much slower pace here than in downtown Manhattan, which is what you are likely to imagine when you think of New York. We made our way there on a Sunday and saw just five or six other people, so a sense of calm and quiet was easily achieved, especially as it had the feel of a cottage garden back home in the UK.

The Alpine House was a complete surprise; a bonus prize in our greenhouse lottery as we didn't know of its existence until we were stood in front of it. The reason for our journey to the Bronx, and to Wave Hill in particular, was to visit the Marco Polo Stufano Conservatory (see page 150) and so to win an additional jackpot in the form of this gorgeous alpine house really made our day.

The current T.H. Everett Alpine House is a recent upgrade on the 1983 original that stood on the very same plot, and is a crisp, clean vision of painted wood cladding and aluminium – the latter really being the star of the show. With the colour of the stormy grey back wall visible through a grid of metal frames, it is reminiscent of seaside chalets or beach huts – only with a New York river view. The new design is impressive as the roof and window panels can all be easily removed, allowing for full control over the internal environment, and yet serving as a protective cocoon should it be required. We liked that the display of the plants inside was a prominent feature – although that is more to do with providing adequate ventilation so that the plants don't suffer from high humidity in the warmer summer months. Whether an intentional feature or not, we found the long expanse of window (albeit window-less when we saw it) to be a pleasing sight.

The hardy alpine plants bask in the sun's rays, huddling in their terracotta pots; half-buried in a heat-moderating bed of sand, they take in all the energy they can just in case the weather turns bad. Native to the rocky outcrops high up in mountainous areas around the globe, alpines are easily mistaken for ordinary wild flowers, and though miniature in size, they are mighty in strength. With the sun falling on the delicate leaves the resulting effect is reminiscent of a trophy cabinet, proudly showcasing highly polished awards and medals for all to see.

COMMUNITY

MEERSBROOK WALLED GARDEN

Sheffield, UK

Although only a few miles away from where we live in the city of Sheffield, Meersbrook Walled Garden has remained a mystery to us until very recently. Once we knew of its existence via a recommendation from a friend a few summers ago, we attempted to see it for ourselves only to find the gate to the garden shut with a locked padlock wrapped around the bars. That was not to be our day.

Originally created to supply food for Meersbrook House (a residential manor house built for Benjamin Roebuck in 1759–60), the potager garden is a small plot guarded by high walls of Yorkshire stone, once yellow, now black, much the same as the house, which still stands about 131ft (40m) away. The parkland around the entrance of the house now belongs to Sheffield city council, and is a space widely used by the people of Sheffield, a so-called 'outdoor city'. There is a long history of influential figures that have fallen in love with the panoramic views over the city's Central Valley that can be seen from up here; J.M.W. Turner painted here in the late 1790s and John Ruskin chose Meersbrook House as the home of his museum. Formerly the Museum of St George but renamed the Guild of St George on relocation, it was established to celebrate nature and its connection to art, and to use that association to empower everyday man. The museum was located at Meersbrook House until the 1950s, when the collection outgrew the space, and was moved to a purpose-built museum at Weston Park just a short distance away. Now there are playing fields, tennis courts and playgrounds for people of all ages to enjoy. The whole park is a significant feature in the city's landscape, as are all the other parks in Sheffield – we are proud of our green spaces.

Having 'Meersbrook?' scrawled on a Post-it note for far too long, and following numerous attempts to make contact with anyone who could allow us access, we decided to take a chance and went one Sunday following a mention of an open day on the Meersbrook Park Users Trust website. The garden is being restored to a vision of its former self by Sheffield City Council, an army of generous volunteers and the staff of Heeley City Farm, a local city farm that champions education within the community and sustainable practices. This time our luck was in and the gate was open.

The garden is cottage-esque – cared-for but definitely not manicured and a little overgrown in places – but in a wonderfully wild way that we really like. We see a mixed group of retirees huddled in an outbuilding, brandishing large white pads of paper and colourful tins of wooden pencils, their hair forming a sea of pale grey in the classroom.

Just past the red-brick outbuilding we find the reason for our quest. The greenhouse is a long dome, curved yet straight at the same time and just about standing up on its own, albeit with a few panes of glass that are somewhat worse for wear. The frame shows signs of rust in beautiful russet tones that are occasionally cushioned by patches of moss in an intense bottle green, and the glass is fogged in places with a thin layer of algae making its way across the surface. To a lot of people this might sound critical, but these are all the things that we love in the place; the subtle signs that nature is claiming the ground back for itself and finding any way it can to assert itself. It also sounds as if we're describing a building that has been forgotten about and again that's not the case. Evidence of craft workshops and community-led activities lie all around us in all their garish plastic glory. Sunflowers sit in pots with children's names neatly written on white labels, a wipe-clean gingham tablecloth is thrown over the table and numerous gloves lie abandoned all around. Initially we dismiss the greenhouse, as our first impression of it lacks the impact of others that we've seen, but as we make our way past the odd pieces of garden furniture we are introduced to an archway of grapevine, its leaves waving to us and inviting us closer. We are used to travelling across continents to visit greenhouse buildings, or being shown one specific climate in great detail, and while desert gardens are very common, tropical hothouses have become a regular experience and we've even seen enough ferneries to fill a whole volume, we've never seen a bog garden and a bog garden is what features here. Consisting of a small shallow pond and a very marshy looking bed, the bog garden is small but mighty. We love the idea that the door might be left open for visiting amphibians to wander in and out quite freely, helping themselves to a refreshing dip and a rifle through the weeds to seek out a decent meal. Indeed, numerous weeds shoot up between the paving stones and nasturtiums glow brightly – weeds here are king.

We see a noticeboard advertising 'Art Days', 'Apple Days' (no idea) and a 'Solar Tea Party' (the same), and despite its dishevelled appearance it is clear to us that Meersbrook is a hub of community spirit. It is clear that even a space as small as this has enormous value to the local area as somewhere to gather, socialize, exercise and engage in activities that people may not have access to elsewhere. And although the greenhouse may be just a small part of the walled garden here at Meersbrook Park, we are sure that the garden wouldn't be quite the same without it.

RAINFOREST BIOME

Eden Project, Cornwall, UK

Holidays to the Cornish coast have become a part of our shared life together: blustery walks along the headland of Trevose; fish and chips at Rick Stein's restaurant in Padstow; and watching the sun set over the waves in Constantine Bay. We inherited our regular holiday destinations from our families (Cornwall and Norfolk respectively), and while endless days burying our siblings in the sand was enough to satisfy us when we were much younger, now we take it upon ourselves to spread our wings a little further and explore the other riches those counties have to offer.

The light in this part of the world is regarded as spectacular, drawing artists and painters into its villages for many decades, with most settling on St Ives as their playground due to its rugged coastline and dramatic topography. Greats such as sculptor Barbara Hepworth, ceramicist Bernard Leach and painter Alfred Wallace have all been vocal about their love for this town as their home, and have all created work here that shows a clear influence of what they saw around them. Fishing villages around the coast of Cornwall, such as Mousehole, Polperro

and Mevagissey, have frequently been the subject of work by predecessors and amateurs alike, with pastel-painted houses, green hillsides and harbour boats as their subjects.

A world away from the Cornish idiosyncrasies, but just 10 miles (16km) up the road from Mevagissey, is a £140 million re-imagination of a disused kaolin (china clay) quarry and at least a week's worth of entertainment for two greenhouse-lovers like us.

Eden Project was conceived by businessman Tim Smit, designed by architect Nicholas Grimshaw and engineered by Anthony Hunt and Associates. Opening to the public in March of 2001 after over two years of construction, Eden emerged from the ground as a series of interconnected giant spheres, like something from another planet. The site consists of beautifully landscaped terraces with weaving paths and zonal planting to educate visitors on the critical importance of nature and what it means to us as humans living on this planet. The buzzing of bees and the scent of lavender fill the air, and the planted beds roll into one another as we advance through the gardens.

The greenhouses, or in this case 'biomes', are separated into two climates, Mediterranean and rainforest, the latter being our natural preference as it is such a dramatic contrast to what we are used to seeing at home. As we glide through the sliding doors at the entrance the rise in temperature hits us and fogs our camera lenses, rendering them useless for a while. As they become accustomed to the 95°F (35°C) heat, we do the same by shedding layers of jumpers and reaching for the water bottles in our bags. The heat is intensified by the humidity required to emulate the rainforest climate, and with the sun glaring down on the thermoplastic ETFE (Ethylene tetrafluoroethylene) structure, it feels a lot warmer.

Built into the remnants of the quarry, the topography of the internal space forms a gentle slope and undulating paths gradually guide us uphill, with suspended walkways and rope bridges, eventually placing us high above the canopy, some 164ft (50m) up. The thick green leaves of tropical plants are packed together, but a little room is left in order for staff to label and care for them, and for ease of public viewing; the primary rainforests of the world are so densely overgrown that it makes finding a way through them a feat in itself (in fact the most dense of Earth's jungles, such as Tortuguero in Costa Rica, are entered only by a few researchers and local inhabitants). A loose division into global regions sees areas representing Southeast Asia with its rice paddies, South America complete with a crashing waterfall, and the islands of the tropics abundant in fruiting trees and nuts.

Our feeling of endearment towards this particular greenhouse stems from our quest to learn more about how life survives in these climates and how plants form symbiotic relationships to help them to do so. The constant fight for light, water and nutrients sees species working with and alongside one another with astonishing ingenuity and this makes for a sight that is rich in texture.

A strong message of sustainability and ecological awareness is threaded into our journey through the Rainforest Biome. Eden is a hugely popular tourist attraction with a visitor count to date of over 20 million, and we hope that each of those visitors learns something of the integral part plants play in our existence, and the relationship we need to build and strengthen in order to continue to thrive on Earth.

THORNES PARK CONSERVATORY

Wakefield, West Yorkshire, UK

Our journey to a park in the south-west of Wakefield in West Yorkshire was made solely to check this place out and we walked tentatively from the car park so as not to mess up our trainers in the muck from the gaggle of geese and ducks that were enjoying the pond.

The original conservatory here was probably built as part of the garden of Thornes House, a Georgian dwelling designed and erected in the late 1770s, for local cloth merchant and politician James Milnes. Although the conservatory that now stands here has done so for a mere 50 years or so, it is a permanent resident of the surrounding rose garden, and has recently been restored to make it a safe place to visit. Built against the original red brick of a walled garden and sat proudly at the head of a formal display of vibrant roses, Thornes Park Conservatory, to us, is a rough diamond.

The whitewashed glass prevents us from seeing inside until we have stepped through the door, and also serves as a protective filter from harsh sunlight; although the plants here are from tropical and desert environments, it is clear that they aren't tended to all that often, which means that regulated growth is probably best. We are greeted by the view of another door some 65½ft (20m) away at the end of an avenue of cacti. Beds on the left are home to Golden Barrel (*Echinocactus grusonii*), and long, rippling ribbons of striped *Agave* tumble all over the place. On the opposite side, a hip-height metal bench runs the entire length of the room,

and sitting on top is a gang of eccentrics, all dressed in terracotta or similarly coloured plastic pots, with the occasional sign warning children about their spikes. They all seem happy enough and show us the occasional pale yellow flower or long stems of flowers that have just come into bloom. We like the haphazard nature of this group and how they all have their own personalities to present, and the simple act of making a garden by bringing containers together is a notion we are fond of. It is wonderfully uncomplicated and keeping the plants in their own pots makes them much easier to care for.

There are another two parts of this conservatory and everything starts to unravel a little once we leave the desert world behind us. The first is, we suppose, a temperate zone, an assumption based on the mountain of jasmine that has taken hold. It is unruly and wild and very dark in colour. In the past we imagine a neat display of pelargoniums and geraniums would have been the focal point of this room. Instead it's a thoroughfare (or a botanical obstacle course) with our reward being the tropical zone through the door just ahead. As it turned out we found this to be more tropical in name than in nature, but in no way did that detract from its charm. Bird of Paradise, *Calathea*, *Ficus* and our beloved *Monstera* all wrestle together here, and though somewhat untidy, together they seem to create that wild jungle aesthetic that we miss in more manicured collections.

In this greenhouse there seemed to be less of a feeling of escapism than we have encountered elsewhere, but more of a sense of resilience and of hardiness; in here the plants are protected from the frost and from the rain, but that is about it. And that is what we think makes it wonderful.

RESEARCH

BOTANISCHE TUIN ZUIDAS

Amsterdam, The Netherlands

Despite holding a collection of more than 8,000 succulents and cacti, we didn't know about the Botanic Garden at the Vrije University of Amsterdam until we were on a tram southbound from the city centre to investigate it. During an Instagram search for something other than the obvious to do while in town, we stumbled upon an image of what appeared to be a mountain of cacti, and we did as much online research as we could to find out if we could see them in person.

Every single one of our expeditions comes with a certain element of risk; we set out hoping to discover something new (to us at least) and to add a fresh angle to what we're doing. Our biggest concern isn't that we won't find a place to our liking, because even if we don't like something, we can appreciate what is different about it and learn from that. Instead the risk lies in the simple reality of access; what if we make our way there and the gates are locked?

In the event, that fear was groundless, and we wandered through the gates at Botanische Tuin Zuidas without a hitch. A youngster in greenhouse terms at around 40 years old, this group of steel-frame structures is no more than average in architectural terms, but more than makes up for it on the inside. A series of 40ft (12.2m) rectangular houses are connected via a corridor at one end, with a door on each house to maintain the temperature inside. Epiphytes, a family of tropical plants that grow without the aid of soil, using the moisture in the air to collect nutrients and are usually found balanced on tree branches, are here in abundance. In fact, everything here is in abundance – packed so tightly together that it is difficult to photograph adequately. Everywhere we turn we are met with *Echeveria*, *Kalanchoe*, *Crassula* and bromeliads galore, and in the next room it is spider plants, peace lilies, and all manner of things that hang from the ceiling with the main aim of tickling the backs of our necks. Further rooms (we lost count how many there are) house philodendrons, orchids and more exotic life, often in multiple sizes, and all planted in deep brown plastic pots. Every single surface is covered, tendrils tumble down and meet others that climb upwards, even filling the space in the middle so there is no room left for anything else – us included.

The jewel in the crown of this greenhouse is the room that we left until last, and it is quite possibly one of the hottest we have been inside to date. The cacti house is a thing to behold with over 8,000 plants living happily inside a relatively small space – it made us think we could probably fit in a few more at home. It didn't surprise us to learn that this is the largest collection of cacti and succulents in the whole of the Netherlands (and for a country so fond of its plants this is a well-earned achievement). This is in part due to the four decades of research that has taken place here; the garden was originally established for the Biology faculty of the Vrije University, and has grown and developed as staff members, students and volunteers have followed their fields of inquiry. Another factor that has contributed to the growth (no pun intended) of the collection is that the botanic garden is required to accept any specimens confiscated by customs officials at nearby Schiphol Airport. If deemed endangered, these specimens are protected, and must therefore be looked after for research purposes. We always wonder where botanical contraband ends up and it's good to know that here at least it is in safe hands.

The packed greenhouses at Botanische Tuin Zuidas are special to us for a number of reasons, one of which is that we understand a little of what it takes to maintain a hundred or so plants, and so can really appreciate the amount of time, expertise and energy that goes into keeping such a large plant family. They are also lesser known than those at the more established Hortus Botanicus (see page 14), and we can never resist an underdog.

ROYAL BOTANIC GARDENS, KEW

London, UK

Kew is probably the place that most people think of when they talk about glasshouses because the gardens' 1840s Palm House is so quintessentially British that it almost hurts. Located in south-west London, Kew was favoured as a summer retreat by successive members of the royal family from the Georgian era onwards. During the 18th century Prince Frederick and Princess Augusta, parents of the future King George III, established a garden around Kew Palace, and in 1759, William Aiton of Chelsea Physic Garden was employed to look after the small 'Physick Garden' at Kew, marking the beginnings of the botanic gardens. Named a UNESCO World Heritage Site in 2003, the gardens now house over 30,000 species of plants, as well as a Herbarium with a collection of 8.5 million preserved specimens, the largest and most diverse plant and fungi collection in the world.

The Royal Botanic Gardens, Kew is an international botanical research organisation and educational institution, as well as a key London visitor attraction. The 997-strong staff roster is partly funded by the Department for Environment, Food and Rural Affairs (Defra), with additional funding provided by donors, membership and commercial activities, including ticket sales.

The 326 acre (132ha) site in Richmond upon Thames boasts a vast Arboretum (covering over half the footprint of the site), collections of bonsai, cacti and orchids, a Rock Garden, a Rose Garden, Rhododendron Dell, Grass Garden, 36 Grade II-listed structures, including the temples of Aeolus, Arethusa

and Bellona, the former residence of the Duke of Cambridge, four Grade I-listed buildings, and what was most interesting to us, the glasshouses.

We could probably have filled the entire book with the various greenhouse buildings at Kew (there are six, not including the nursery and collections greenhouse range, which is for more specific research projects and not open to the public), with another 18 in the garden's past that have since been demolished – with the plants moved to various points around the site to join other collections.

Our first love at Kew is the Princess of Wales Conservatory, with its wonderful straight lines that break up the curves of the foliage, and give us an interesting view at each point along the inside of the greenhouse that covers 48,427sq. ft (4,499sq. m) Most of the space is divided by clean, black-framed rectangular panels of glass, and we move from the Mediterranean to the Dry and then to the Wet Tropics, all under one incredible roof. We are acquainted with orchids, philodendrons, bromeliads and, during the summer, enormous waterlilies. Designed by Gordon Wilson and opened in 1987 by Diana, Princess of Wales, the building won the Europa Nostra Award for conservation; the climates inside are controlled by computer, allowing for incredibly efficient energy management.

Personally, we love the variety on show here and the ability to wander from one continent to another; we could spend all day hiding in the many levels that form the topography. We like that there is hidden seating and we always photograph the same spots when we visit, noting the changes and developments of the plants. An area we especially love is the fern room, a sort of in-between atrium area defined by heavy concrete blocks that just show their faces through the foliage, with an opulent finish provided by the silver accents of the handrails on the level above.

Another world entirely is the iconic Palm House that is just a short walk from the Princess of Wales Conservatory. While it lacks in area, it makes up for it in personality, and although it is half the size of the Temperate House, still around 16,000 panes of glass make up the roof. When it was constructed in the 1840s by iron founder Richard Turner (who built it to Decimus Burton's designs) the glasshouse was the largest of its kind and thus the engineering was particularly innovative; borrowing techniques and materials conventionally used in shipbuilding, the silhouette takes on the shape of an upturned boat and, especially when viewed from across the Palm House Pond, it appears to float just above the ground. A heavy wrought-iron framework makes up the skeleton of the structure, and is visible both inside and out. Its painted white veins run through the palms and cycads, flowing into the serpentine staircases at each end and back onto themselves.

A 62ft (19m) walkway surrounds the central hall and allows visitors to look down onto the treetops and feel truly immersed in the jungle. We have noticed that the Palm House has the inexplicable ability to swallow up time, and we think that no matter how busy the glasshouse is, it never feels as if we are sharing it with anyone other than the lush green leaves that create giant arches high above our heads. Fan palms wave at us enthusiastically and the tropical blue-greens of Bird of Paradise cool the hot and humid air (the temperature in the summer can reach 104°F (40°C).

For us, the conservatories at Kew are less about the individual details, and more about the entities as a whole. They represent the ideas and design principles originally defined by the glasshouse greats John Loudon and Joseph Paxton, and act as a legacy to the tremendous work they both did in the advancement of horticulture in the Western world.

Kew's contribution to the world goes much further than attracting tourists and its upkeep is far more than simply honouring the tradition and history of the garden. It is a centre for global research and at the very core of Kew's existence is a quest for knowledge and understanding about the natural world and what that means for the future ecology of the planet. In learning about plants and fungi, the science initiatives at Kew hope to outline potential strategies for conservation, environmental policy and even treatment of life-threatening diseases. It is much more than just a pretty face.

THE GLASSHOUSES

University of Oxford Botanic Garden, Oxford, UK

The glasshouses at the Oxford Botanic Garden are a collection that is particularly close to our hearts. They were the first that we visited and must have made quite an impact as we haven't stopped talking about them since.

One cold but sunny Sunday, we found ourselves to be the first eager visitors to the garden, so early in fact that we had to wait for the glasshouses to be opened. The low morning sun sparkled as it filtered through the glass structure and we watched as botanical shadows were cast softly on the ochre walls.

The seven glasshouses that sit between the winding course of the River Cherwell and the original 17th-century stonework of the walled garden are a stunning modern addition; a Hartley Botanic construction they are made up of aluminium straight lines and exotic interconnecting worlds.

Palm-lined corridors lead us through each climate, starting with the Cloud Forest that makes us think of dinosaurs and the origins of the Earth. Great fronds unfurl in front of us and appear as full-colour versions of Karl Blossfeldt's photographic studies; trailing Spanish moss (*Tillandsia*) seems to drip from the ceiling, as staghorn ferns (*Platycerium*) reach out to us with friendly fingers. The air is damp but warm, and the scent of the wet earth that has become symbolic to us as a place where man and nature intertwine, filters through our lungs.

There is an eerie atmosphere in the space that follows: Venus flytraps (*Dionaea muscipula*) lie in wait, the tubes of trumpet pitchers (*Sarracenia*) sit open-mouthed in readiness for their next meal, while great fleshy pitcher plants (*Nepenthes*) hang heavy with inviting sweet nectar; meet the inhabitants of the Carnivorous Plant House. Despite the dark feel we like it in here. We can sense the power held by the plants and appreciate the quiet air of violence – survival of the fittest and not just the prettiest.

The mood lightens in the tropical Lily House as the space is dominated by a huge tank (the oldest original structure on the site, built in 1851, which is full to the brim with lilies and semi-aquatic plants. There are leaves of all shapes and sizes; discs of stars, frilly foliage and strands of tiny, delicate flowers, while the showstoppers are the great lily pads of *Victoria cruziana*, a close relative of *V. amazonica*.

Our final meeting in Oxford is with the desert plants in the aptly-named Arid House. Cacti wrestle with the glass ceiling and cause us to reassess what we know about the tiny versions that we have on our windowsill

at home, while the strong, silvery leaves of *Agave* appear to slide across our vision and point elegantly to the various lumps and bumps of cacti and succulents on the floor. This room is full of spines and needles, and has the same dark feeling as the carnivorous plants, only this time the botanicals are acting purely in self-defence.

Out in the open, the air is instantly cooler, the light is a little harsh, the ground soft underfoot. A glance back at the glasshouses is pleasing; green leaves squashed against the panes in an effort to get closer to the sun, although we know that if they ever broke through, they – like us – would wish they were back in the comfort and safety of their man-made home.

The gardens at Oxford were founded in the 1600s with the aim of 'Sharing the Scientific Wonder and Importance of Plants with the World', and that mission statement still stands today. The glasshouses play a huge part in helping to educate by allowing the possibility of different climates in which plants can thrive, and we certainly think they have managed to make nature appear glorious. This is somewhere you can study, observe, and while away the hours in a pocket-sized exotic location.

PLEASURE

ROYAL BOTANIC GARDEN EDINBURGH

Edinburgh, UK

Including the glasshouses of the Royal Botanic Garden Edinburgh was an obvious choice. The difficult part came when we tried to decide on what our focus might be, and as the areas open to the public consist of no less than ten gigantic glasshouses we regard it as a 'complex' rather than just a single entity; to emphasize just one aspect posed a near-impossible task. We reminisced about our very first visit some years ago when we had braved the pouring rain, stopping only for a brief moment at the towering *Gunnera* (a member of the rhubarb family, Polygonaceae), which lined the pond at the entrance to the historic gardens. A winding path steered us through grass lawns, punctuated by interesting trees, which at that time were dressed in their autumn colours and decorated with glistening water droplets – Scotland is notorious for its inclement weather and on that day it was no different. We were in Edinburgh for a weekend away and to add a new city to our travelogue, although the only thing that was definitely on our agenda was to see what the Royal Botanic Garden had to offer.

The answer to that was more than just a place to while away a few hours, but instead was the beginning of a new relationship, however mawkish that sounds. That first trip was the first of many and hopefully there are many more still to come. We've added a four-hour trip and an overnight hotel stay onto a journey just to have a few hours there; we will jump at any opportunity to visit and tend to recommend the garden to anyone and everyone planning a jaunt even vaguely in the direction of Scotland.

Nearing the glasshouses that very first time, we see a futuristic expanse of glass panels and a zig-zag, spider-like exoskeleton of steel frame. This, we later learned, is the most recent addition to the range that has been added to and adapted since the very first Tropical House was built in 1834. The entrance to the glasshouses is a little further on and requires you to pass the sci-fi-esque design and gaze at the moisture-laden fronds that caress the steamy panes. This is the point where man and nature meet, and we love to get lost in the visual treat this coalescence creates, like falling into a painting.

Through the first building (dating from 1858), a rather grand looking stone Victorian affair comprising tall arched windows and a curvilinear glass top, we head indoors. Inside, palms grow both tall and wide in equal measure, native to southern China and Australia but seemingly very happy here in Scotland, wrapped snug under a greenhouse blanket. Passing through the doors we enter the oldest member of the Edinburgh glasshouse family; an octagonal turret, built in 1834 to recreate a tropical rainforest environment, it is home to tall bamboos, towering fishtail palms and the elderly sabal palm which out-dates even the oldest glasshouse here.

Moving through a glass corridor into the 1960s addition, with less stonework and more glass, we head into the rest of our afternoon, which is spent exploring the six different 'rooms' that represent the different climates of the world; from the hot and humid world of orchids and cycads, through the peaceful, cool air of the fernery, and into the harsh, arid desert.

Ferns and Fossils is a room of grandparent plants that reference what the world was like millions of years ago. It is a cool, calm and quiet place to be and everything drips – we are in a cloud forest on a hillside somewhere in Australasia. We weave our way through the mossy landscape, position ourselves in front of a mass of concrete that is formed into a raised bed, and stand still for a while contemplating our view. This concrete corner was especially constructed to house a mass of *Equisetum myriochaetum* (horsetail) and for some reason we find it mesmerizing. We find extraordinary that it has been given its own little area; it grows so rampantly that it would take over if allowed to run free with the other ferns, and we've seen its English cousins do just that in the low-lying fields near our house.

Perhaps it's the cool air that reminds us of wet woodland walks together, the soft carpet of vibrant green *Selaginella*, or the tranquil sound of the shallow stream passing through the rocks that we like here, whatever it is it keeps pulling us back to that particular spot.

The Plants and People House is dominated by a huge 18,038-gallon (82,000-litre) elliptical pond that is surrounded by food-providing tropical plants. Being a hot and humid room, we have no choice but to stop in here for a while and take stock of our surroundings; our lenses have fogged and take a while to recover. We use this time to investigate the lush *Monstera* that is climbing one of the end walls and comment on the incredible size of its glossy leaves. Other plants provide the chance for visitors to learn about the economic importance of bananas, rice, sugar and cocoa. The real showstoppers in here, and always winners in our eyes, are the gigantic lily pads of the *Victoria* 'Longwood Hybrid' – a slightly hardier relative of the famous *Victoria amazonica* that has made such an impact on glasshouses all over the world. We have witnessed the flowers of these plants here countless times and it's always a pleasure. Being lovers of foliage, their sheer size always makes a huge impression.

If you were to press us for a definitive favourite part of this place, we would have to leave the glasshouse complex, return to the outdoors and make our way around to the lower level of the Temperate Lands glasshouse, which is accessed through an atrium decorated with umbrella trees (*Schefflera*) not unlike the ones we have at home. A concrete bridge spans the length of this room, and joins the Plants and People house to Rainforest Riches at first-floor level, making a heavy architectural statement as soon as we walk in. Vines cascade over the edges of the structure, catching the light on their starry leaves so they look like Christmas decorations. Under the bridge it's dark and gloomy but somehow feels comforting rather than threatening – there is no way of knowing whether the plants are growing up from the ground or down from the sky, which makes us feel swaddled in green. Windows flank the right-hand side and tendrils reach out to grab any light that they can, sometimes disturbing the condensation on the glass and sending droplets running down the pane. Whether it is a ghost town that has become overrun by nature, or a futurist utopia where all of the world's inhabitants co-exist, this small greenhouse ignites cinematic scenes in our heads.

CLOUD FOREST

Gardens by the Bay, Singapore

Words escape us when it comes to describing the Cloud Forest at Gardens by the Bay, a nature park, garden and tourist attraction in the Marina Bay area of Singapore. It's somewhere we think should be experienced first-hand – it really can't be adequately explained using language and is even difficult to do justice in photographs.

Possibly the newest of all of the stops on our greenhouse tour, the Cloud Forest is one of two conservatories that opened to the public in 2012, designed by architects WilkinsonEyre, and the two structures morph out of the water like sea creatures that have come to rest in the South Bay Garden. Gardens by the Bay form part of a government initiative to increase the quality of life of the people of Singapore by populating the city with green spaces and they attract millions of visitors each year.

We had a short conversation before we approached the automatic doors of the conservatory, having already stood underneath the Supertree Grove (actually much smaller in real life than we thought it would be, but no less impressive) and it dawned on us that we may have unrealistic expectations about what we would find inside this greenhouse, especially one that we had just endured a total of 15 hours flying time to see.

Although we had seen other people's images, and had read extensively about what we would find here, the fact remained that we didn't really know what we were going to see and whether it would enthral us in the way we hoped. All we knew for certain was that the Cloud Forest Dome is home to the world's highest indoor waterfall, and that the room temperature is somewhere in the region of 75°F (24°C), but we had no idea of the internal layout, or just how much that temperature would impact on us, despite it only being a few degrees lower than outside the dome.

As we walked through the turnstiles and the doors beyond, all our concerns disappeared. The waterfall stands at an incredible 115ft (35m) and fills our vision completely, throwing a wave of cool air over us, as well as a light mist of water. The vapour tingles as it meets our warm skin and we feel the full effect as a refreshing contrast to the air outside. The awesome power of the cascading water is demonstrated by an immense noise as it crashes into the pool below, causing us to shout excitedly to one another. We spend a while underneath the towering mountain, straining our necks while gaining a sense of the climate of the cloud forest.

Lying at the centre of the dome, the 'mountain' consists of 2,577 panels of glass cut into 690 different shapes that cover an area of over 129,167sq. ft (12,000sq. m), and aims to replicate the environment found somewhere between 1,000 and 3,000ft (305 and 915m) above sea level – such as those found in the tropical mountain areas of Southeast Asia and Central and South America. The true cloud forest is so named due to the persistent low cloud cover (its meteorological term is 'silvagenitus') that floats in the canopy as a result of the hot conditions that cause the moisture in the vegetation to evaporate. Typically, the few areas in the world where the altitude is sufficient to allow a cloud forest to form are rich in mosses, epiphytes, ferns, lichens, bromeliads and orchids – and the Cloud Forest Dome in Gardens by the Bay is no different. The walls are alive with variations of begonia and maidenhair fern that offer innumerable colours and textures; deep dark green ovals next to pointed silver and purple, with delicate white petals punctuating the display, the pattern continuing as far as the eye can see, until it is disrupted again by great arrows of *Anthurium* and the appetizing droplets of Rose Grape (*Medinilla magnifica*). The majority of the plants that adorn the mountain itself are epiphytic (meaning they don't require soil in which to grow) and perch quite happily on their man-made pedestal.

The arrangement of the greenhouse is based around a one-way system that begins at the top of the mountain amongst the pitcher plants (*Nepenthes*), Venus flytraps (*Dionaea muscipula*) and sundew (*Drosera*), and winds downwards through the mist-filled Cloud Walk and along the Treetop Walk. This brings you out towards the edge of the dome, allowing a great vantage point over the Secret Garden below, via a suspended metal walkway. Weaving in and out of the mountain on different floors provides varying vistas, and the intricate silhouettes of exotic plant life drip their way through the material structure. From the inside it feels as if the plants are slowly making their claim on the mountain and building their own utopian dream.

At the foot of the mountain we find ourselves in the Secret Garden, which is an ode to the planet's rarest plants that once grew in abundance and now much less so, due to the loss of their natural habitat and the changing climate of the Earth. Here we find the Wollemi Pine, native to Australia and listed as 'Critically Endangered', which although it was only discovered in 1994 is a species thought to be around 200 million years old. Here it sits in the colourful company of many gingers, heliconias and more begonias (so many begonias!) as well as the strikingly varied faces of the many different anthuriums – some dark and velvety with strongly defined veins, while others are more rounded and less threatening to the eye.

This particular greenhouse is a very special place for us, because we understand something of the effort and expense expended in order to achieve such a lifelike rendition of the real-life cloud forest, a climate we have been lucky enough to experience for ourselves for a short while in Costa Rica and which was an experience we will never forget. We are drawn to the views that contain both human and natural elements because we are fascinated by the blurred line between these two worlds, and the Cloud Forest Dome is a perfect example of unbelievable engineering and outstanding attention to detail from a horticultural perspective. So much love, research and expertise has gone into forming this giant centre for edutainment and we can only urge others to experience it for themselves. Ultimately, the purpose of the greenhouse is to entertain and to inform, for people to take away a view of the planet that is more sustainable, and to build a generation that feels responsible for the Earth and its future. As with most of the greenhouses we visit, sustainability is high up on the list of priorities and here rainwater is collected from the curved roof, fed into the cooling system and connected to the Supertree Grove, which also happens to form the vents for the greenhouses. This continuous ventilation helps maintain the humidity while keeping the air fresh and restricts the unwanted growth of algae and fungus.

There is certainly an art to creating an immersive environment, and the sheer scale and success of this whole operation is unlike anywhere else in the world, and is, quite frankly, mind-blowing.

ENID A. HAUPT CONSERVATORY

The New York Botanical Garden, New York, USA

We visited The New York Botanical Garden in the Bronx on a sunny Saturday in the summertime, which in hindsight might not have given us the best chance of seeing the conservatory as empty as we would have liked, and indeed it appeared that most of the world had decided that they quite fancied joining us on our tour that day. It was busy, but definitely not so much that it wasn't an enjoyable place to be, and it was easy to find a quiet corner away from the crowds, but perhaps slightly more difficult to document without a few photobombs from fellow greenhouse admirers.

Originally established in 1891, the Botanical Garden had quite a romantic start in life, as the idea was heavily influenced by a honeymoon trip to the Royal Botanic Gardens, Kew (see page 96), which Nathaniel Lord Britton and his wife, Elizabeth, very much enjoyed. The couple, who were both botanists, were particularly inspired by Kew's Palm House and also by Joseph Paxton's Crystal Palace, and brought their experiences of both grand glasshouses back to New York with them.

Leading greenhouse manufacturer Lord and Burnham was the company tasked with the design, and the total construction cost was $180,300. With their knowledge and expertise (they also built San Francisco's Conservatory of Flowers (see page 26), Volunteer Park in Seattle and the Phipps Conservatory in Pittsburgh), they created a design in the Victorian style and the conservatory opened in 1902. With its wrought-iron frame and curvilinear glass it is easy to see the influence of Kew's much-loved Palm House, and based on the foot traffic on the day of our visit, the people of New York clearly love it too – more than a century later.

In 1978 the greenhouse was renamed after publisher and philanthropist Enid A. Haupt, following the donation of a substantial sum to repair the building ($5 million for the work and a further $5 million for ongoing maintenance). The project also involved restoring the conservatory to its original design, which had been compromised during previous renovations in 1936 and 1956. Of course, it is near impossible for us to picture the past but having seen even the simplest of greenhouses turn to dust in local fields, we can only imagine that repairing a building of such size and complex engineering must have been an incredible undertaking.

We make our way around the predefined route, which ensures you pass through all of the different sections and displays; the building is split inside into eleven different pavilions separated by double doors, making the transition from one climate to another much more manageable than within a single, free-flowing space. We have become accustomed to wandering around greenhouses in whichever way takes our fancy, and this kind of structure (with a fully-booked tour going on at the same time) meant that we take a little more time to enjoy each area than we usually do. At one point we decide we want to take a second look at something and make our way back to the previous pavilion – we get a true sense of what it is like to swim against the tide.

The glasshouse at The New York Botanical Garden is similar to many other greenhouses, with its ornamental outline and grand, Victorian-inspired curves, emphasized by the whitewashed glass that helps to filter out the harsh sun and provide a little more shade indoors. It holds a number of different stages of tropicality in terms of plant life, from lush rainforests through to the dry desert, and yet the buzz and life that moves through the glass walls feels very different from those elsewhere – it is much louder and perhaps more animated. That's not to say that we didn't like it, in fact it encouraged us to seek out the quietest spot we could find (in the Upland Tropical Rain Forest Gallery), and that feeling of solace remained with us as we made our way back to the train station.

Coincidentally, just on the other side of the fence that divides the railway from the road, was a garden. Not a big garden, or anything ornate, but a small, humble vegetable plot that was ripe with tomatoes, peppers and all manner of salad leaves. We overheard someone on the platform making a snooty comment about this 'pathetic attempt' compared to what was on show at the Botanical Garden. Granted, it was a bit scruffy around the edges, and certainly not an RHS Show Garden, but it was still someone's creation and one that was quite obviously cared for. While we are also guilty of visiting the greats, this helped us realize that we can bring a little of those grand greenhouses home with us, and interpret them for ourselves.

TROPICAL GREENHOUSES

Planten un Blomen, Hamburg, Germany

The story of our visit to these greenhouses comes with a minor hiccup. We planned our journey to Hamburg specifically to see them and set a ridiculously early alarm to make our flight. Two hours or so after take-off we exited an underground station via a short escalator and were greeted by the sight of a second-hand bookshop tucked into the station entrance. In the yellow light of the display cabinet we saw a 1941 edition of Karl Blossfeldt's *Urformen der Kunst* (*Art Forms in Nature*) for €180. Suppressing the urge to look inside at old books that we didn't need, we turned back to the task in hand and stepped into the Alter Botanischer Garten, which was just to our left. Standing at the foot of an empty stream in need of an umbrella, surrounded by acers changing into their autumn wardrobe, we followed the signs to Tropengewächshäuser and our common sense and basic German told us that we were moving in the right direction.

The rainfall became heavier but nevertheless we withstood the deluge to spend a little time taking it all in. The Tropical Greenhouses have been the main attraction in the park since they were built in 1963 and the building has since been listed. Interestingly, the five conjoined greenhouses are built into Mediterranean terraces (also listed) that lead down into a canal, and today that canal was full, and the large, cold raindrops continued to fall. Constructed almost inside-out to prevent any internal obstructions, the view of the greenhouses is dominated by a moody grey framework of zig-zag steel. Multi-faceted, like a round-cut diamond, the greenhouse stood out to us for its contemporary appearance. Through the amber-coloured beech trees we spied banana leaves squashed against the glass, creating a cloud of condensation. As the condensation builds, each droplet joins another and slowly makes its way further south before picking up enough pace to form a small river that races to the floor, ending in a puddle on the ground. The winding rivulets appear as the beginnings of a new language – perhaps a message to invite us inside.

The Succulent House is different to any other we've seen: a long gallery of a room, flanked on the window side by a continuous trough, planted up with *Crassula*, *Echeveria* and cacti. Opposite there's more of the same, only on a much grander scale, where giant skyscraper cacti huddle together almost like a big city seen from afar. At the base of this high-rise landscape is a rolling carpet of Golden Barrel (*Echinocactus grusonii*) and *Kalanchoe*.

A backdrop of grey concrete boxes becomes a waterfall of trailing plants, each trickling into the next; in a few years' time they will form a delicate succulent curtain in striking contrast to the heavy blocks used as the base.

It was the first time we had travelled to and from a different country in a single day and it made the world feel a little smaller. The aforementioned 'hiccup' appears beyond the bizarre Farnhaus (fern house) and through the subtropical regions exhibited in the Schaugewächshaus (show greenhouse), and comes in the form of a printed notice on the door to the Tropengewächshäuser. It reads, 'This part is today closed for renovation. Please accept our apologies.' We stand in front of the glass doors and consider the journey we have taken: our winding drive across the Pennines in the dark hours of the morning; a plane, several trains and a short walk to find ourselves unable to see what lies on the other side of that door. We peer into the green abyss beyond and imagine the size of the leaves that live there, the tangling world of tropical life with its tall palms and climbing philodendrons.

It is probably the most breathtaking greenhouse we've never visited, simply because we weren't able to get inside. We walk away, mumbling about how great the rest of the building is, and justifying our day to one another – it was absolutely worth it but it's always satisfying to know we've left no stone unturned in our greenhouse quest. On this occasion, however, we might have to omit the 'tropical' from the Tropical Greenhouses of Hamburg, but perhaps one day we will return for the full experience.

BARBICAN CONSERVATORY

Barbican Centre, London, UK

The conservatory here is remarkable to us for many reasons, but most of all because it is almost like walking onto a film set, or that we're seeing a glimpse into the future – a place where nature and urban development have come to some kind of equilibrium. Here is the ultimate utopia as the rugged Brutalist structure of the Barbican is softened by its collection of over 2,000 tropical plants and trees.

As the second largest greenhouse in London after the Royal Botanic Gardens, Kew, the Barbican Conservatory provides a true inner-city oasis to those that visit, and can do so without paying an entrance fee, providing a continuation of that utopian, 'for the people' ideal and something that we value greatly.

In great contrast to the garden at Kew, the Barbican Conservatory has no such research agenda or horticultural programme to follow, but instead serves as a place for pleasure. Visitors are invited to explore the multi-level walkways on Sundays and take afternoon tea on Bank Holidays, surrounded by leaves. It's not unusual for us to see a sketch pad in use, or excitable children on the look-out for the orange flash of the koi carp in the pond, and although we have visited many times before as members of the general public, on this occasion we were given access outside the usual public opening hours. We feel very lucky indeed and this is the only public place we visited on our tour where we received special access. It was strange having the whole place to ourselves and we imagined what it would be like if we had something of this scale at home for us to enjoy exclusively. On reflection, we realize it would probably be a huge amount of work to maintain such a healthy family of houseplants, so we are happy for it to stay in the public realm and to let other people enjoy it.

The conservatory opened in 1984 as an addition to the already established Barbican Estate, designed by Chamberlin, Powell and Bon, and was constructed around the theatre's large fly tower (used for storing stage sets) as a way of concealing it. From the inside, the imposing structure and its cascading greenery has a way of making us look up, like the arches in a church, or the tree trunks in a forest leading to the canopy silhouetted against a bright sky.

The bold, heavy architecture and sub-tropical planting here are a winning combination for us, ticking many of our 'if-we-ever-build-our-own-house-it-will-look-like-this' boxes. We admire the use of humble unforgiving materials, such as raw concrete and earth-coloured brick, and the bold decision to keep these exposed, rather than to hide them away. It brings a certain element of unapologetic honesty to the surroundings, and puts simple, basic materials on a pedestal, with the 2,000 tropical plants used in the indoor garden all forming part of the same celebration.

Looking at old photographs of the space (some are now pinned to the noticeboard outside the manager's office, which is a small purple-brown box cleverly disguised underneath a clambering vine) it is interesting to see that nothing has really changed in almost 30 years, aside from a great deal of growth. The tumbling leaves of *Tradescantia* hang over the edge of the balconies and reach towards tall *Ficus* branches that come up from below, joining forces like Michelangelo's *The Creation of Adam*. The leaves of *Philodendron* fill the cavities between great chunks of coarse grey-blue, palms fight their way to the roof and brushed brass letters spell out 'The Conservatory'. An alluringly pale variegated Swiss cheese plant (*Monstera deliciosa*) reaches up the white powder-coated steel columns, making full use of the criss-cross formation as a botanical climbing frame. This is our first encounter with a variegated version of our old favourite and we manage to track one down for our own home as a result.

The Barbican Centre itself is a lively hub: it is a performing arts venue with a gallery, a library, cinema screens and three restaurants, playing host to music concerts and theatre performances all year round, but our favourite production is the silent movie that sits on its roof.

MARCO POLO STUFANO CONSERVATORY

Wave Hill, New York, USA

We knew that Wave Hill might be a shrinking violet compared to the boisterous character of The New York Botanical Garden and we chose to visit the former first, perhaps to provide a way to centre ourselves before heading into the crowds of the more well-known garden just a few miles away.

Noted for its two houses and 28-acre (11.3ha) garden, Wave Hill has been open to the public since the mid-1960s, after a long history of noteworthy connections. Some of the estate's famous associations include writer Mark Twain, a young Theodore Roosevelt and Thomas Henry Huxley, who worked closely with Charles Darwin. Built as a country home in the 1840s by landowner and lawyer William Lewis Morris and added on to over the years, Wave Hill House is listed on the National Register of Historic Places.

From 1866–99 Wave Hill was owned by William Henry Appleton, a publishing scion with a healthy interest in the natural world, who developed the gardens and was responsible for the erection of the first glasshouses on the site. By 1903, the property had been purchased by George W. Perkins, a partner at J. P. Morgan, who extended what was then the main house, today known as Glyndor Gallery, by adding a swimming pool and improving the garden with terraces, additional greenhouses and a recreational facility that still stands today, and now houses the Ecology Building. It was during Perkins' time at Wave Hill that the landscaping of the garden took on the shape that it holds now, with the addition of contouring, a variation in levels and lawn areas defined from more planted beds. In 1926 the house was struck by lightning and suffered heavy fire damage. It was demolished and the building that stands now was built in its place to a design by architects Butler and Corse.

In 1960 the Perkin-Freeman family gifted the Wave Hill estate to the City of New York and a non-profit organization was formed with the intention of celebrating, protecting and continuing the garden's legacy. Given the impact that it had on certain names in its past, it is true to say that Wave Hill has played a huge part in forming strong relationships between visitors and nature, and though this took place only on an individual basis, it is impossible to measure the wider implications of those bonds.

The Marco Polo Stufano Conservatory is fronted by a beautiful flower bed that bursts with texture and animated colour; we enjoyed the relaxed form of the gardens here, especially in the blur between formal hardscape and informal planting. It felt like an organic place that is controlled more by nature than by human design, and when outdoors that is always something we look for.

Inside, the conservatory is split into three, with a Palm House in the centre, a Tropical House on one side and a Cactus and Succulent House on the other. The Tropical House is captivating because it reminds us more of a nursery than a typical tropical house, although of course that is only really defined by the plants that live inside. The neatly organized benches hold a great selection of plants – each one different and unexpectedly smaller in stature than those usually found in larger greenhouses. The colour palette of lime greens and pale blues is also surprising, with accents of terracotta orange that bring a feeling of warmth.

This greenhouse is charming, like a sweet shop, filled with plump, healthy succulents, dripping from the ceiling and spilling over the edges of the troughs.

HOBBYIST

PRIVATE CACTI COLLECTION

North Yorkshire, UK

Midway up a country lane sits a grand old house of red brick – not just the everyday brick that many of the UK's terraces are built from, but that old red sandstone of grand Scottish castles. Our memory is somewhat distorted, so in our minds the house resembles something you might find in the Highlands rather than the quaint North Yorkshire village that it sits in. A gravel driveway rolls out from the open five-bar gate, which is propped open with a block of white-painted stone, and a sign reading, 'Cacti for sale; please drive in.'

An extension lead guides our car up the drive, like a bright orange line drawn with a giant crayon, which separates the pebbles from the part-trimmed privet hedge. Attached to the extension lead is a hedge trimmer held by a tall, distinguished gentleman who greets us with a warm smile.

Visible over a yet-to-be-tamed section of the privet are a dozen or so squares of glass fixed at jaunty angles with aluminium trimmings, and as more panes come into view, we see the unmistakeable shape of a Hartley Highgrow 10 greenhouse. Originally erected in the 1960s this particular glasshouse has obviously lived a colourful life, but protected from the elements by its nook in the garden, this veteran has stood the test of time. The shape of the Hartley is undeniably distinctive and its space-age silhouette is one that we've become familiar with on our greenhouse journeys.

Inside this greenhouse (one of three that live here) we become more closely acquainted with our kind host. Some say that the spaces that we create are a window into our minds, and if this is the case then this one belongs to a wonderful human being; it is overflowing with knowledge, and although it might appear disorganized at first glance, it is a vision of orchestrated chaos when we take a closer look. A bearded clump of *Mammillaria* (a member of the cacti family) is nestled in the fluted arms of a Mother of Thousands (*Kalanchoe delagoensis*), which has thrown its plantlets into any pot that will take them, and subsequently become a modest, purple-toned forest. The star of the show in our opinion is the waterfall of Ghost Plant (*Graptopetalum paraguayense*) that topples over the edge of the bench, its dried flowers still floating around the silvery starbursts of its rosette formation. Succulents are a great love of ours and here they are in abundance. We like them because they look full and fruit-like. Essentially, a succulent is the plant version of a water tower, and by serving as their own reservoir, they appear plump and juicy, which is very pleasing to the eye.

We made friends with the corners of the two largest greenhouses, one set for display and for sale (with the proceeds going to charity via an honesty box) and the other, sitting a little further back into the plot, for propagation. On one shelf a card reads, 'Private Collection', and we can't help but admire the unsteady script of all the signs. The world needs more people in it that are trusting enough to invite others into their world and make sure they are looked after, even if they can't be there to welcome them in person; long live personal touches, honesty boxes and handwritten notes.

The second greenhouse is a miscellany of cacti and their children; this is the nursery side of the operation

and comes in a colour palette of racing green, faded artichoke and varying shades of burnt orange. Plastic pots, well-used potting trays and re-purposed ice cream tubs form the internal building blocks and shelves are stacked high with them; each tray or container is a project-in-progress and the outward sign of a deep horticultural interest. Our cacti collector tells us how he started with one for each of his children, way back when they were somewhere between toddlers and teenagers, and that (no pun intended) the collection just 'grew from there'. We learn of his commitment to his hobby as he points out his favourites, reeling off their Latin names as if it is the most natural thing

in the world, and finds us examples of plants he has adopted from friends and since propagated into newer versions to be sold onto visitors like us, forever filling that pot of money for the charities he sees fit to receive his donations. Undoubtedly there is a glue that holds everything together here, filling the greenhouses with character and ensuring that the life continues inside, despite our host being in his nineties. He is single-handedly responsible for creating this beautifully wild world here in North Yorkshire, and we can only thank him for it – and perhaps take a few cuttings home to broaden our own private collection that might one day inspire others the way he has inspired us.

ABBEY BROOK CACTUS NURSERY

Near Matlock, Derbyshire, UK

We have visited Abbey Brook Cactus Nursery many times over the last four years and it never fails to bring us warmth and a cactus souvenir or two to add to our collection at home. It was the first cactus nursery we ever visited and it immediately won our hearts with its character and charisma.

Situated on a 4 acre (1.6ha) sloping plot, overlooking the green and expansive Derbyshire Dales, Abbey Brook has been the site of husband-and-wife team Brian and Gill Fearne's nursery since 1976, after they outgrew their original site in the garden of Brian's mother's home in Sheffield, just 20 miles (32.2km) away.

On this visit, and on many visits before, we were waved down the driveway by Gill, who always seems happy to see visitors, and makes sure we know where everything is. It's laundry day and we are aware of this because clothes are hanging out to dry on the line next to where we park our car. Little details like that make this place what it is, and also helps us to appreciate that, not only is the nursery a business for Brian and Gill, it is also their home.

The nursery consists of four greenhouses, two of which are open to the public. The other two are off limits, but that doesn't stop us from attempting to peek inside as we walk past. Grapevines dominate one of these greenhouses, and the other is full of anything and everything that we've ever wanted to see – or at least that's what we imagine because we know that we are unlikely ever to get the chance to go inside. However, once we enter the greenhouses we are allowed to visit, we pretty much forget about the others, and don't feel as if we're missing out on anything at all.

The main greenhouse is the retail house, and desert plants of numerous types are sat waiting patiently to find new owners. An island runs along the centre, with a cashier desk to the front, and a staff-only area towards the back that is cordoned off with a beaded curtain. Plants are labelled and priced individually, based on their size, rarity and the ease in which they can be replenished. Also for sale is Brian's own personal mix of cacti soil and we buy a bag, as well as some gravel, which we top the soil with. Brian taught us a while ago that this helps prevent anything rotting, aids drainage and goes a way to creating the desert aesthetic in our home.

Throughout the greenhouses there are plenty of identification labels and interesting facts, but most importantly there are care instructions in the form of the four basic rules of looking after cacti and succulents. This is the Gospel according to Abbey Brook:

FOUR BASIC RULES:
1. Water once a week in summer
   (March until end of September).
2. No water in winter.
3. Place in full sun.
4. Protect from frost in winter.

Obviously, it can be a little more complicated than that, but we appreciate that the first step towards making a garden is to know the basics and we love that Abbey Brook is keen to educate.

Most of our time here is usually spent in the neighbouring greenhouse that is home to their six National Collections: *Lithops*, *Conophytum*, *Haworthia*, *Mammillaria*, Abbey Brook *Echinopsis* hybrids and *Gymnocalycium*. A mouthful of complex Latin but an eyeful of joy in simple terms.

The appeal of these greenhouses lies in the passion that the Fearnes hold for their plants and their dedication to maintaining the collections. Looking after them not only requires skill and organization in order to the keep the specimens alive, but being part of the National Collection scheme means they must record everything meticulously. By recognizing the value of what they have, and protecting it through such a scheme, they are ensuring the legacy of those plants and adding to the wealth of knowledge that we have about the natural world. We can't help but think that without curious minds and dedicated spirits like the Fearnes, we would all be a little lost. Brian himself has dedicated his life to the study of *Lithops*, a small group of succulents that resemble lifeless pebbles or stones in an attempt to avoid being eaten. *Lithops*, or living stones as they're commonly known, are native to Namibia and South Africa, so it is a testament to Brian's hospitality that they are so happy here in rural Derbyshire.

DIY ALLOTMENT GREENHOUSE

Sheffield, UK

We don't have to travel far in the UK to find allotments; in fact, we can step out of our front door right now, and walk to three different sites within a few minutes. The history of allotments dates back to Anglo-Saxon times, but the more recognizable version was established in the 1900s. These small plots have played a large part in forming (and feeding) modern culture in the UK. Originally intended as a way to help those that were unable to afford to buy food, land was shared out to the masses in an attempt to help the population to grow their own vegetables, thus improving diet, family finances and, in a more holistic view, the country in general. In the 1920s, legislation was introduced to regulate the plots, and today there are several hundred thousand allotment users across the country.

In most cases, the land is owned by the local council and managed through a society or association. A series of rules and criteria must be met when renting a site, such as the ones local to us. The main one of these is that 'at least 75 per cent of the total plot area must be used to cultivate fruit and vegetables', and our favourite, 'Greenhouses count as space used for cultivation, provided that they are in use.' This means that our suburbs sparkle when we rush past them on the train, and our raised vantage point allows us to peer over hedges and gaze at the flotilla of sheds, polytunnels and greenhouses that sail on a sea of cabbages, leeks and runner beans.

Allotment mentality is a wonderful thing: it is the art of making do with what you have and being inventive with empty yoghurt pots, discarded window panes and old scraps of carpet. We admire the lack of consideration for appearance that makes the haphazard and low-fi aesthetic entirely organic, and we think it all the more beautiful for it, in some way reminding us of the potted street gardens that can be seen all over Tokyo in Japan.

One particular allotment site, a birthday gift to its custodian, caught our eye. Sitting on a sloping site overlooking the south side of Sheffield, is a DIY structure that resembles a miniature version of the Pinterest-famous cabin built in West Virginia by artists Nick Olson and Lilah Horwitz. It is also not dissimilar to Jesse Schlesinger's *Sunhouse (ii)* (see page 194) and is a real-life greenhouse that performs true greenhouse tasks – that is not to display plants, but with the aim of helping to *harvest* them.

We are welcomed at the gate by our host and her 'littlest lady', a one-year-old named after her parents' favourite Roald Dahl character, and seems to have adopted similar personality traits as her namesake as she sits quietly observing our escapades through the hedgerows, pointing every now and again at nothing much in particular. Negotiating the pram wheels over the grass proves tricky but it doesn't seem to be a sensation altogether unfamiliar to our chaperone as we are told that she is a regular supervisor here. We learn of the task of gathering PVC windows from people that were giving them away, of the surprising ease with which everything joined together, and the plans to improve the greenhouse. When we talk to gardeners or plantspeople, we always find that they have plans – no garden is ever finished, it seems, but is a constantly evolving entity, and of course we never ever seem to visit at the right time. We are frequently told that the biggest, most impressive flowers that ever were have died just two weeks ago, and that next spring is definitely when it will all 'come together', and this visit is no different.

We have come right at the end of the summer season, and consequently also at the tail-end of the veg-growing season; cucumbers had finished perhaps a week before and the tomatoes still on their vines will probably not ripen before the temperature and light levels start to fade. Undeterred we continue through the old wooden front door that probably began life on one of the terraced houses nearby, and the chequerboard pattern of the greenhouse comes into view. Constructed for a budget of next-to-nothing but rich in character, the DIY greenhouse sets an example to those who wish for an indoor/outdoor garden space, but don't have the finances to attempt a Grand Design.

To this young family, the allotment is an extension of their home; it is a place for sanctuary, nurturing of the soul and a form of social engagement as it connects them with other allotment-holders around them. It allows them to become part of nature in a physical sense by moving their hands through the earth, and provides a greater connection to the concept of time and even magic as 'you just put things in the ground and they grow'. The low-fi greenhouse stands proudly at the head of the allotment, serving as a nursery for seedlings in spring, a tomato house in summer and shelter for those days when the rain makes an unscheduled arrival. We trust that the quiet 'littlest lady' in the pram will watch her parents rotovate, plant and harvest their potager garden for years to come and develop similar skills, growing to love her place in the world, and more specifically the make-do greenhouse that lives on the hillside.

ARCHITECTURE

THE KIBBLE PALACE

**Glasgow Botanic Gardens,
Glasgow, UK**

True to its reputation, Glasgow treated us to a day of pouring rain and so our approach to the city's Botanic Gardens is a flustered one. Huddled under a single, black, half-broken umbrella, we bump into one another as we make our way along the wet streets, past immaculate Georgian tenements and heavy Saturday morning traffic. Our conversation is more focused on whether we will end up with a parking ticket than our expectations of what we might find in the garden ahead of us – that and the struggle of sharing one small umbrella between us.

Fortunately, the rain eases slightly as we pass through the 19th-century gates, and we happily discard the umbrella, slow our pace a little and look up to see the gardens in front of us. Turning to our right we are confronted by the mysterious frosted domes of the Kibble Palace, which are to be our destination for a few happy, precipitation-free hours.

Much Googling tells us that the glasshouse standing before us is, rather oddly, an exaggerated version of its former self. Originally built in the 1860s as a private conservatory at the home of inventor and engineer John Kibble, the structure (at the time called the Crystal Art Palace) was at the centre of a bizarre agreement that resulted in a complicated number of changes in ownership and management responsibilities, as well as a complete upgrade and relocation from the shores of Loch Long to its new home in the West End. Before now the palace has served as an exhibition and concert venue for up to 6,000 people as well as being a teaching/research facility for the University of Glasgow.

Fast-forward 130 years, what is now known as the Kibble Palace has undergone a further £7 million, three-year refurbishment programme to restore its original architectural elements, and give the building a defined sense of purpose.

Slightly distorted yet colourful shapes move on the other side of the milky glass and drift around the entrance like aliens, eventually coming into focus as raincoat-covered figures; inquisitive tourists like ourselves, squealing children, or people taking refuge from the weather that has interrupted their Saturday stroll.

Passing through the main doors we immediately turn left into what we assume to be one of the 'arms' of the building, intrigued by the sign that promises 'Killer Plants', and into the carnivorous room. A sea of slightly drab green plants lies in front of us, consisting mainly of fluted, upright *Sarracenia*, low-lying ferns and sun-bleached moss. A waist-level bed lines the outside curve of the room and guides us around a central bed, both planted with various insect-eating specimens that invite us to look closer. Tiny droplets of sticky glue perched on the end of delicate leaf blades play with the light as we move past, the abundance of textures in the beds serving as a feast for our eyes. The more we look into the miniature moss world the more we seem to see – similar to the way in which our eyes adjust to the night sky and we begin to see increasing numbers of stars.

Under the main dome of the Kibble Palace lives a National Collection of tree ferns from Australia and New Zealand, some of which date back to the 1880s. We follow the lines of their deep brown trunks down into the ground and then out again as they seem to reappear in a different direction to form another tree. A bright green carpet of *Fittonia* and other damp-loving greenery spreads itself across the fernery floor, occasionally gaining height (and hopefully sunlight) as it scales the tree trunks. Fronds unfurl in front of us and throw out curly fingers to touch the moist air, while those that aren't yet ready stay curled in tight spirals and remind us of the cinnamon buns that we once ate for breakfast in a café in Berlin – a strange connection, but that's how the world and our minds seem to work.

Wandering through our much smaller, slightly more Scottish version of Jurassic Park (some fern fossils are approximately 360 million years old), we move from deep shade into small pools of light and stand directly below the circular centre of the roof. Looking up we see hundreds of panes of glass, all in different sizes and overlapping one another. This place is full of curves and circles, highly decorative ironwork details and fancy twisting columns; on paper, it is not particularly to our taste, but in practice it all seems to work together and we find ourselves wanting to forgive the Victorian ornateness.

Our exit from the glasshouse takes us via a room that mirrors the first carnivorous area, only this time it houses cacti and succulents, as well as the remnants of a weekend club meeting that had taken place just prior our visit. Plastic chairs and a few stray desks are piled up in a corner ready to move into storage until next week's class. A single bed pushed against the wall is home to various cacti and succulents that would normally live in the warmer temperatures of the Mediterranean; aeoniums and aloes creep along the makeshift ground, all pointing their strange little heads to the sky above.

Architecturally, we can't recall having been into any other building quite like the Kibble Palace. Although we have stood inside many Victorian creations held together with cast iron frames, elaborately decorated and fancy fretwork below our feet, the defining feature here, we think, is the glass. The thousands of translucent panes of glass enclose you inside a kind of wondrous bubble and protect you from the outside world – which, in Scotland, tends to be wet with rain. As you walk through the doors it is as if you are transformed into alien-like shapes (as it seemed to us when we first arrived) taken on a prehistoric journey and ushered back out again in the flowing current of other visitors.

ADELAIDE BICENTENNIAL CONSERVATORY

Adelaide Botanic Garden, South Australia, Australia

As we had travelled over 10,000 miles (16,000km) to see the Bicentennial Conservatory in the Adelaide Botanic Garden, we'd put ourselves under a fair amount of pressure to enjoy it. It was about to pour down with rain (again) and so we were quite glad to see this strange spaceship appear in front of us. In the event, it turned out to not be a spaceship at all, but rather a modern (1988 is quite recent in greenhouse terms) vision of elegant silver steel and 26,199sq. ft (2,434sq. m) of toughened glass that is apparently referred to locally as 'The Giant Pasty'. Whether an extraterrestrial vehicle or a baked food stuff, it's fair to say that this particular conservatory is one of a kind, and we included it in our tour because it comes with a story that we think teaches a good lesson.

Designed by South Australian architect Guy Maron, it is the largest single-span greenhouse in the southern hemisphere, and was created to house super tall (65½–131ft/20–40m) palm trees. The design has won numerous awards, including a Royal Australian Institute of Architects Award of Merit (1990), and is one of the youngest buildings to be listed on the South Australian Heritage Register, a record of areas, places or related buildings that hold significant heritage value to the state. The curved form of the building allows rainwater to run off easily so it can be collected and utilized in watering, as well as helping to guide condensation on the inside away from the canopy.

When it opened in the 1980s it did just that, and provided a tropical rainforest climate, and more specifically one with very high rainfall all year round. The plant life consisted of trees, palms and tropical specimens from Papua New Guinea, Indonesia, northern Australia and the Pacific Islands, all of which thrive on constant warmth and high humidity.

On our visit, during the Australian winter, we are surprised to find that the conservatory isn't much warmer than the temperature outside, which was about 59°F (15°C) – not exactly the comforting warmth we were expecting. Confusingly, a large glass panel standing just inside the entrance promises a temperature of a rather warmer 77°F (25°C). The panel also features facts and figures about depleting rainforests around the world, but ironically this acts as a signifier of the change that was to take place at the conservatory.

It transpires that some time in 2012, due to rising energy costs and falling budgets, the decision was taken to remove the more delicate tropical plant species and turn off the heating altogether. This benefits the botanic garden by saving a great deal of money and allowing visitors free admission due to a reduction in running costs, but crucially it also acts as a perfect analogy of how fragile ecosystems like this can be, and just how threatened the world's rainforests are by shifts in temperature.

Once inside, guided by a twisting path, we explore the upper walkway first that enables us to find our bearings and to make sense of where we are. Slender, ochre-coloured palm trunks dissect the green vista and lead our eyes upwards to the curving roof and then back down again along another trunk to the 'forest' floor below us. Dodging pools formed by occasional drips from somewhere above us we meander back on ourselves, now at the lower level, and are able to admire the creeping lianas that wrap themselves around whatever they can

find to get that little bit closer to the sun. All around us we see palm grass (*Molineria capitulata*), ferns and other vivacious green foliage. It is very jungle-like, and at times it even feels very real because it is so tangled and uncouth, but because of the cool temperature it certainly doesn't feel very tropical!

We do encounter small hints of the exotic, however, rooted in the leggy anchors of the pandanuses that stand in the dark water of the pond, filtering through the torn fishtail palms and in the sight of heart-shaped taro leaves.

TROPICAL DISPLAY DOME

Brisbane Botanic Garden, Mount Coot-tha, Queensland, Australia

At the foot of Mount Coot-tha (but still at considerable altitude) are Brisbane's Botanic Gardens. In 1974 a second attempt was made to create a botanic garden for the city, as the original site had been flooded a total of eight times in 100 years, and the city council felt it appropriate to establish a bigger, better version of the popular garden site that was less prone to flooding. The first gardens, now known as the City Botanic Gardens, remain open to visitors and are located in the central business district (CBD), by the banks of the Brisbane River, where they have been since 1855.

Mount Coot-tha is so-named because *ku-ta* (honey) produced by the native stingless bee was collected here by Aboriginal Australians, and this is where we found ourselves on a local bus, zig-zagging our way up to the summit in the hope of seeing our first geodesic greenhouse dome aside from those at Eden Project.

Although we visit in the early spring, the weather is pleasant enough to be wearing just a single layer, and we find the air to be warm with just the slightest remnants of winter present in the form of a light breeze. The established 138 acre (56ha) gardens feature over 200,000 plants from all over the world, and we enter through the Arid plants region; a landscaped area alive with bright umbers and fiery reds bursting out from a swarm of *Aloe* and *Lampranthus*. As the garden slopes downhill the distinctive shape of the Tropical Display Dome comes into view like a beehive, with energetic visitors buzzing in and out of the entrance.

Inside the dome the honeycomb appearance consumes us as it is reflected perfectly in the near-still water of the lagoon-like pond and echoed once again in the shadows cast by the aluminium frame onto the hard floor. The triangular latticework makes a really graphic backdrop to the silhouettes of the tropical planting and we find ourselves taking the same photos over and over in an attempt to take it all in; it is unlike any other greenhouse we've ever been in ... but we do tend to say that about them all!

The dome allows the display of exotic plants that wouldn't grow freely outdoors in Brisbane but instead favour the conditions created by being located a little closer to the equator. Plants such as the dark and mysterious *Anthurium magnificum*, the velveteen *Philodendron micans* and a tree with the most spectacularly shaped leaves, *Trevesia palmata*, which are native to Colombia, Mexico and Vietnam respectively, wind their way around the central pond and act as our guides.

It's not a surprise to us that the Tropical Display Dome has become the great symbol of the Brisbane Botanic Gardens as its shape can be easily recognized from a distance. Next to the pond an etched metal plaque features a beautiful quote by the British author and conservationist Gerald Durrell and we thought we'd end our account of the Tropical Dome with his words:

'Our ark is the air, water, land; and all the species of plants and animals, including ourselves are the crew. How can we be so blind as to continue our acts of sabotage?'

SUNHOUSE (ii) AT GENERAL STORE

San Francisco, California, USA

In the back garden of the lifestyle shop General Store in the Outer Sunset, San Francisco, is a small, sun-bleached shed. It's a shed that is essentially a pile of old windows and discarded timber that came together (with a little help from artist Jesse Schlesinger) to make one near-perfect home for a beautifully ramshackle collection of cacti and succulents.

Jesse's installation entitled *Sunhouse (ii)* is planted in a truly Californian garden: chunky weathered wood seating that comes with a comforting fragrance after being gently warmed all day by the sun; a low-maintenance pebble lawn and grasses that rustle in the salty air blowing in from nearby Ocean Beach; while agaves and aeoniums line the borders and form a path that guides us to the tall, thin reclaimed door.

Opening the door reveals an oddball group of inhabitants – myriad different pots sit on two levels of shelving, three if you include the ground. Their custodians are a mixture of cacti, *Euphorbia* and *Kalanchoe* in all shapes and sizes (with a few elkhorn ferns and the occasional overflowing *Senecio* succulents too), housed in rusty old tin cans and plastic containers, as well as terracotta and ceramics, perfectly complementing the pastel tones and washed-out textures of the surrounding garden and the painted houses of San Francisco. The plants themselves are full of character, a little rough around the edges, and most of them share their planters with a few sprigs of would-be weed *Oxalis* and a spider's web or two.

We had seen *Sunhouse (ii)* (as we have so many of our favourite greenhouses) on social media, and walked quite a distance (even after flying a few thousand miles) to stand inside it for ourselves. It could be that we fell for the low-fi mentality of this pint-sized, plant-filled shack, or that we'd walked 10 miles (16km) of undulating San Francisco hills by the time we reached this place, but we sat for a while to enjoy it. Something about this particular greenhouse wooed us; it felt like an achievable goal and an object of beauty in its own right, perhaps even more so because of the once-rejected materials it was made from. We like that Jesse gave these pieces of timber the time of day and created an elaborate jigsaw in his bid to connect them all together in a way that would make a suitable shelter.

CACTUS STORE
(HOT CACTUS POP-UP)
New York, USA

Around a graffiti-covered corner on the outskirts of Manhattan's Chinatown lies Cactus Store, a temporary but sturdy-looking steel-frame greenhouse filled with hundreds of odd-looking cactus characters. The simple structure sits snugly in a gap between two buildings and its translucent plastic panels reveal almost nothing of what can be found within – it is one of those 'if you know you know'-type places, like a treehouse club with a secret knock to gain entry, or a cloak-and-dagger bar where you enter through a fake wall in a barber's shop.

We wait outside for a while for the other visitors to thin out and note the intrigue of passers-by; couples lingering on the sidewalk trying to peer past us, assessing whether further inspection is necessary. Admittedly, if we had stumbled on this place by accident, we probably wouldn't have realized that it was here, and would have waltzed on with our day unawares.

This pocket-size greenhouse is a New York City pop-up version of a long-established store in Echo Park, Los Angeles, and is run by friends Max Martin, Carlos Morera and Jeff Kaplon. The line-up on the shelves (a custom powder-coated steel frame in a moody grey tone with rough-cut timber planks) consists of a much more exotic collection than you would find in your average plant shop.

Cactus Store is a mecca for those that really know what they like; each specimen is far from that idealistic shape we've seen in a million emojis, but instead represents nature a little more truthfully. Gnarled and twisted, this motley crew of cacti and *Euphorbia* are sourced in the Californian deserts and carefully curated here to find homes in the apartments of New Yorkers who are seeking to reconnect with the natural world, no matter how odd-looking that association might be. They celebrate the imperfections that are earned in the plant's effort to survive the desert environment, and as a result present a display that is rich in character and charm – not so much luscious and jungle-like but more of a sense of a life well lived. These plants are like our elderly grandparents with a few stories to tell and we love to listen. Strange, misshapen and sometimes just plain rude, the shapes of these cacti are probably politely described as 'sculptural', but there is an ugly/beautiful paradox at play and we salute the passion that Martin, Morera and Kaplon plough into their projects.

This interest in and appreciation for what is a somewhat 'unconventional' beauty is something that becomes infectious and it is clear to see that this has been the case here as the store has been an undoubted success. Even the gravel used to top the soil is to be envied; a mixture of colours and sizes it gives the whole setting of the plants a feeling of real authenticity.

The Echo Park store is very LA: a neon 'Open' sign sits in the window; the lop-sided plants are perched on Brutalist cinder blocks; and a Dodge honks outside the open door at the complacent driver who has paused at the nearby traffic lights. Here in New York on the other hand, the pop-up is a more refined establishment and blends seamlessly into the rich tapestry of its Manhattan home. Our time here is short and sweet, but like all the best treehouse clubs, we leave feeling as though we have been allowed access to one of New York's secrets, and we come away smiling, knowing that we have been a part of something special. The very act of Cactus Store 'popping-up' means that by the time this book is published, it will most likely have ridden away into the sunset over this iconic skyline, leaving a trail of pastel gravel and a city full of new cactus custodians.

THE STEINHARDT CONSERVATORY

Brooklyn Botanic Garden, New York, USA

We arrived at Brooklyn Botanic Garden late on a Saturday afternoon after our first day exploring Manhattan, which gave us a few hours to get lost in the conservatory in the glorious golden light, and we took to it so much that we were the last ones in the conservatory when the garden closed. It is highly likely that the reason we ended up spending such a long time in Brooklyn's largest greenhouse was because of the way it incorporates underground levels into its design, and the resulting rabbit-warren feel. Completed in 1988, the Steinhardt Conservatory is one of the most interesting we found in terms of its internal layout.

The main entrance is at ground level and connects through separate greenhouses at this stage both to the left and right of the entrance chamber. Just beyond the main entrance is a wide staircase, which takes you down to a subterranean level, with a further three greenhouse pavilions connected by a central underground hub. In person, we lose track of what is up and what is down and quite how we got there, and to be honest it doesn't really matter at all.

The greenhouse as a whole is a very *green* place (that may sound obvious, but many conservatories tend to be planted up with colour), and on a hot day we found the abundance of foliage to be refreshing. There are rich silky *Anthurium*, *Monstera deliciosa* leaves larger than our heads, and cycads that thrust themselves into the walkways.

We particularly love the Desert Pavilion and spend far too long in here; the warmth emanates through the milky glass, oblong windows, configured in a way we've not seen before, almost like an emerald-cut diamond. The Desert Pavilion is home to the plants that derive from arid regions and are split into 'old world' and 'new world' categories. The 'old world' refers to places such as Africa, Asia and the Canary Islands, while the 'new world' includes the Americas – so-called because before America was discovered geographers believed that the eastern world was all that existed. The plants are nothing particularly new to us, but the examples are well maintained and obviously very cared for. It is funny how we can sense the level of care and attentiveness just by how a plant grows, but we have a good feel for it now, and here everything is free from cobwebs, each lump of gravel is in its place and pots are free from dust despite their sandy setting. Tall stacks of cacti shoot upwards, and the light glows through the hairs making them almost luminescent, while others snake along casting wide shadows on the ground.

We take our time here and comment on the similarities to the *actual* deserts we had seen just a few days before. The Joshua Tree and Death Valley are both very different environments and although it is tricky to create somewhere like a desert when you only have a limited amount of space, the planting really gives a good idea of the feeling of the landscape, even though it is a much more compact version.

We also love the Aquatic House and have to be shooed out as the conservatory closes. We discovered it with about 15 minutes viewing time left and we did all we could to drink in the view. In here a ground-level pond forms the basis of the pavilion and the surface of the water is almost completely covered with greenery and foliage; mangroves spring from underneath, along with the tiny leaves of water spangles (*Salvinia*), papyrus and, of course, many waterlilies. Something about the light holds our attention, and everything appears gold and green, painted by the afternoon sun.

SHINJUKU GYOEN NATIONAL GARDEN GREENHOUSE

Tokyo, Japan

We found Tokyo to be a world apart from our expectations; it wasn't noisy or intense and didn't even seem particularly busy. Perhaps using Hollywood movies to prepare us for our trip was a little misleading, or it could be that we just ended up in the quieter spots without realizing it ... either way, Tokyo was more of a shock to our system because it was less of a shock than we were expecting. We thought we would need designated rest stops in between rush hours and a taste of wilderness to remind ourselves that there is more to life than the concrete walls of the world's most populated city. But we didn't because, as it turned out, Tokyo is a peaceful place and just, well, beautiful.

On our second day in Japan's capital city we awoke to the sound of pouring rain and, as our time in the country was short, we had no choice but to don our raincoats, arm ourselves with umbrellas and make the most of our 6,000 mile (9,656km) journey across the globe.

We glided through the metro system – already self-proclaimed pros after just 24 hours' experience – and looked at each other with furrowed brows as the escalators emerged into the 'real world' at street level; heavy rain poured as only it can in a subtropical climate, and filled the roads in front of us. At one point it looked as if water was shooting up from the ground, rather than falling from the sky, because of the velocity of the bouncing rain. Everyone around us, however, was perfectly composed, and didn't appear to have a drop of water on them – whereas we were utterly drenched and by now somewhat distressed about our bedraggled state. Regaining our composure, we headed off to seek shelter in what used to be the grounds of the Naito family residence.

The greenhouse in Shinjuku Gyoen National Garden became our refuge and we expected to find many others with the same idea. Instead, we shared the giant glass structure with only around eight others, and one of those was a pied wagtail.

The layout inside takes us on something of a journey; at first there is not much to see in the way of plant life until we're guided through a well-manicured fernery contained between walls of dark slate. It is a box-within-a-box that makes us think that there must be more in store to warrant such a huge building – the Jun Shinozaki design contains approximately 2,700 species, including tropical and endangered plants. Our suspicions are correct, and around one more wall of slate we see a bridge over a world of water, with blue-green tones that echo Monet's palette.

The stillness of the water brings calm and induces us to be quiet, as though we have entered a church or temple, a combination of sleek architecture and the natural elements. Every now and again a droplet falls from the geometric steel above and disturbs the surface of the pond, sending ripples across the water to meet the edges of a lily pad. Bliss.

TOUR DIRECTORY

ASIA

Japan
Shinjuku Gyoen National Garden Greenhouse
11 Naitomachi
Shinjuku
Tokyo
160-0014
www.env.go.jp/garden/shinjukugyoen/english

Singapore
Cloud Forest
Gardens by the Bay
18 Marina Gardens Drive
Singapore 018953
www.gardensbythebay.com

AUSTRALASIA

Australia
Adelaide Bicentennial Conservatory
Adelaide Botanic Garden
North Terrace
Adelaide
SA 5000
www.environment.sa.gov.au/botanicgardens

Tropical Display Dome
Brisbane Botanic Garden
Mount Coot Tha Road
Toowong
QLD 4066
www.brisbane.qld.gov.au/facilities-recreation

CARIBBEAN

Barbados
Orchid World
Sweet Vale
Barbados
www.orchidworldbarbados.com

EUROPE

Denmark
Ny Carlsberg Glyptotek Winter Garden
Dantes Plads 7
1556 Copenhagen
www.glyptoteket.com

Germany
Tropical Greenhouses
Planten un Blomen
Botanischer Garten der Universität Hamburg
Junguisstraße
20355 Hamburg
www.bghamburg.de/foreign-visitors

The Netherlands
Botanische Tuin Zuidas
Van der Boechorststraat 8
Amsterdam
www.botanischetuinzuidas.nl/english/

Hortus Botanicus
Plantage Middenlaan 2A
Amsterdam
www.dehortus.nl

United Kingdom
Abbey Brook Cactus Nursery
Old Hackney Lane
Matlock DE4 2Q
www.abbeybrookcacti.com

Barbican Conservatory
Barbican Centre
Silk Street
London EC2Y 8DS
www.barbican.org.uk

The Camellia House
Yorkshire Sculpture Park
West Bretton
Wakefield WF4 4LG
www.ysp.org.uk

Glasshouses
Chelsea Physic Garden
66 Royal Hospital Road
London SW3 4HS
www.chelseaphysicgarden.co.uk

The Glasshouses
University of Oxford Botanic Garden
Rose Lane
Oxford OX1 4AZ
www.botanic-garden.ox.ac.uk

Kibble Palace
Glasgow Botanic Gardens
730 Great Western Road
Glasgow G12 0UE
www.glasgowbotanicgardens.com

Meersbrook Walled Garden
Meersbrook Park
Derbyshire Lane
Sheffield S8 9EH
www.meersbrookpark.co.uk

The Nursery Greenhouses
Forde Abbey and Gardens
Chard
Somerset TA20 4LU
www.fordeabbey.co.uk

Rainforest Biome
Eden Project
Bodelva
Cornwall PL24 2SG
www.edenproject.com

Royal Botanic Gardens, Kew
Richmond TW9 3AE
www.kew.org

Royal Botanic Garden Edinburgh
Inverleith Row
Edinburgh EH3 5LR
www.rbge.org.uk

Tatton Park Fernery
Tatton Park
Cheshire WA16 6QN
www.tattonpark.org.uk

Thornes Park Conservatory
Denby Dale Road
Wakefield WF2 8QE
www.wakefield.gov.uk/sport-and-leisure

NORTH AMERICA

USA

Conservatory of Flowers
100 John F. Kennedy Drive
San Francisco
CA 94118
www.conservatoryofflowers.org

Enid A. Haupt Conservatory
The New York Botanical Garden
2900 Southern Boulevard
Bronx
NY 10458
www.nybg.org

Marco Polo Stufano Conservatory
T.H. Everett Alpine House
Wave Hill
West 249th Street and Independence Avenue
Bronx
NY 10471-2899
www.wavehill.org

Moorten Botanical Garden
1701 South Palm Canyon Drive
Palm Springs
CA 92264
www.moortenbotanicalgarden.com

The Steinhardt Conservatory
Brooklyn Botanic Garden
990 Washington Avenue
Brooklyn
NY 11225
www.bbg.org

Sunhouse (ii) at General Store
035 Judah St.
San Francisco
CA 94122
www.shop-generalstore.com

INDEX

'Haarkon began as an outlet for us to share the things that we collected on our "days off" from our photographic commissions and it has gradually become our entire world. We love to learn, to travel to places new to us as well as re-visiting the familiar and we like to share our view with the world via our website and now, through this book.

Our goal was to create a working life that we could share and we never imagined that we could have so much fun doing it; Haarkon has taken us all over the world and we never ever live the same day twice – something that we are always appreciative of.'

ABOUT HAARKON

Magnus Edmondson and India Hobson are photographers based in Sheffield and together form Haarkon. The pair have a talent for story-telling through their images and have built up a healthy client list including *The Telegraph*, *Observer Magazine*, Sonos, Ikea, Food 52, Made.com, Ally Capellino, JJJJound and Matches Fashion.

The Haarkon blog and social media channels have themselves gained a great following (the @haarkon_ instagram account gained over 200,000 followers in just a couple of years) and has yielded partnerships with Apple, Bang & Olufsen, Carlsberg, Urban Outfitters and Nest.co.uk, as well as travels with the Visit Costa Rica, Visit Copenhagen and Visit Barbados tourism boards. *Elle Decoration* UK featured the Haarkon Greenhouse Tour in their 'Power of Plants' issue, they were listed in Condé Nast Traveller's '32 Travel Instagram Accounts to Follow' and they also sat on the judging panel for the RHS Photographic Competition 2018.

www.haarkon.co.uk
Instagram @haarkon_

THANK YOU

To our family for encouraging us to do what makes us happy, for your unconditional support in our somewhat unconventional career choice and for smiling and nodding at us as though it's a normal thing to travel the world in search of greenhouses. We appreciate that you give us the freedom to be who we are.

To the charities, educators, businesses and individuals that welcome us time and time again into your greenhouse arms. Your hospitality is always much felt and we can't thank you all enough for allowing us to celebrate your work so openly.

To the countless number of gardeners, horticulturalists, volunteers and enthusiasts that work tirelessly to maintain the plants inside the greenhouses that really make the experiences what they are. Without your hard work and vision the buildings that we visit would be without such life and soul.

The Camellia House is featured by kind permission of Bretton Investment Partnership Limited.

To our online community; we appreciate every single one of you. It's incredible that we can connect with people from all over the world and call many of you friends – thank you for inspiring us constantly and for helping us to continue to do what we truly love.

To Krissy, you are wonderful and we couldn't have made this book without you.

To Katie C, thank you for seeing what we see and for believing in us and our odd ideas.

To Laura, Katie H, Claire, Sarah and everyone else at Pavilion that has contributed to *Glasshouse/Greenhouse*; we are so proud of it and so thankful to you guys for helping us make it what it is.

To all of our friends for not forgetting about us even though we're hardly around, to Helly for plant-sitting for us at a moment's notice and to Nick for telling literally everyone you've ever met that we're doing what we're doing. We think you might be our biggest fan.

Finally to Luke. Thank you for listening to all of our ideas right at the very beginning and for pushing us to take the first steps on our journey, even though we didn't really know where we'd end up.